THE GREATEST
SELF-HELP BOOK

IS THE ONE WRITTEN BY YOU

THE RISING CIRCLE

We are a wellness community here to uplift and support your inward journey
by fostering high vibrational living.

Like a circle, there is no start or end to our spiritual journey.

We continue to expand and grow. And as the sun rises every day, so does the light
within us – the same light that illuminates the world we live in.

As a community, we believe we can collectively rise and shine together to create
a world filled with compassion.

Follow us on Instagram and TikTok @TheRisingCircle

Sign up to our weekly newsletter on www.therisingcircle.com

Get in touch via hello@therisingcircle.com

THE GREATEST
SELF-HELP BOOK

IS THE ONE WRITTEN BY YOU

Vex King and Kaushal
The Rising Circle

bluebird
books for life

First published 2022 by Bluebird
an imprint of Pan Macmillan
The Smithson, 6 Briset Street, London EC1M 5NR
EU representative: Macmillan Publishers Ireland Ltd, 1st Floor,
The Liffey Trust Centre, 117–126 Sheriff Street Upper,
Dublin 1, D01 YC43
Associated companies throughout the world
www.panmacmillan.com

ISBN 9781035005185

7 9 8

A CIP catalogue record for this book is available from the British Library.

Design and typesetting by Heather Bowen
Illustration p. 7 © Wheel of Emotions, The Junto Institute for Entrepreneurial Leadership, INC.
Illustrations p. 67, 115, 147, 227 © Eriko Shimazaki.
Illustrations p.10, 11, 87, 123, 175, 179 © Global Creative Learning.
All other illustrations by Heather Bowen, Lindsay Nash and Shutterstock.
Printed and bound in China

Visit **www.panmacmillan.com/bluebird** to read more about all our books
and to buy them. You will also find features, author interviews and
news of any author events, and you can sign up for e-newsletters
so that you're always first to hear about our new releases.

This journal is dedicated to you.

*Now is the time to self-explore, rewrite your story
and become a better version of yourself.*

You've got this.

Journaling is your avenue to emotional literacy.

There is no greater self-help book written than the one you write about yourself.

VEX KING

My name is

and this is my story.

A MESSAGE JUST FOR YOU

We are proud of you for beginning this journaling journey. This journal is truly the best self-help book you will ever experience. I have been journaling for nearly two decades, and it has completely transformed my outlook on life, all while supporting my personal growth journey. I owe much of who I am and what I do today to the daily practice of journaling.

On the other hand, Kaushal has had her fair share of struggles with remaining engaged while journaling – yo-yoing on and off for several years. With my natural love for self-exploration and journaling as an avenue to self-understanding and expansion, along with her experiences and creativity, our mission was to innovate the way we journal. Inside, we have included the perfect mix of questions, activities and proven techniques to help you live your best life. Together, we believe we have created a simple yet exciting journal that offers all the elements necessary for you to rise to your greatest potential.

It brings us so much joy to share this creation with all of you. We hope it sparks as much joy for you as it has for us.

With love,
Vex

CONTENTS

JOURNALING 101

Everything you need to know about journaling

WHY JOURNALING?

According to a study from Queen's University in Ontario, Canada, the average person has over 6,000 thoughts a day. Without knowing, we can hold on to some of these thoughts, allowing them to affect our mood, actions, and the way we speak to ourselves and others. Furthermore, repetitive thoughts can shape our beliefs and all that we can become.

Journaling helps you understand *you*. It places you in the position to observe the activities of your mind. One of the biggest benefits of journaling is that it helps you to become more self-aware. There is power in putting pen to paper. It allows you to reflect on your emotions, how you handle situations, your relationships, and what may or may not be working for you in your life. With regular journaling, you are able to choose more positive responses – those that are aligned with the person you wish to become. This helps you build a healthier relationship with yourself and with others, too. All the while, you shape your destiny through more empowering choices.

WHO IS JOURNALING FOR?

Journaling is for everyone (we mean it!). No matter what you are going through in life, journaling gives you the power to improve your relationship with yourself, and it helps you write your story.

WHEN TO JOURNAL?

You can journal whenever you feel like it, at any time. There is no right or wrong way to journal. You may find yourself filling some sections out in the morning and some before bed. Feel free to grab a hot drink, light a candle, play some meditation music in the background, or do something that helps you get into the zone. Always remember to journal in a way that works for you!

WHERE TO JOURNAL?

Journaling can feel like a daunting task. What if someone reads it? What if you are left feeling exposed? What if it upsets someone? The best thing we can recommend is to journal where you feel safe and supported by your environment.

BENEFITS OF
JOURNALING

Increases your sense of gratitude

Helps to process and regulate your emotions

Can aid in shifting a negative mindset/thought pattern into a positive mindset

Tracks your personal growth

Helps you find your voice

Can help reduce anxiety

Helps you understand what your triggers are and how to better respond to them

Provides a safe space for you and your thoughts with no judgement

Helps increase your self-worth

Provides a space for releasing your emotions

Can turn many of your life experiences into life lessons

Helps in maintaining a routine

Increases emotional intelligence

Is an act of self-love

HOW DO I USE
THIS JOURNAL?

A simple step-by-step guide on how to use this journal

TODAY IS

Start each entry by writing down the date. By doing this you can go back to see how you were feeling on that specific day. Looking back on your entries is a great way to see how far you have progressed!

TODAY IS *Wednesday 11th May 2023*

I WELCOME ALL FORMS OF LOVE INTO MY LIFE

AFFIRMATION

The words we say hold so much power over how we feel. After the date, read the daily affirmation out loud five times for maximum effect!

HOW AM I FEELING TODAY?

There is a heart in the centre for you to colour in. Think of this heart as a visual representation for how you are feeling on that particular day. Use a colour that resonates with you on that day. This is a beautiful way to express how you are feeling without using any words. It is also great to look back on and track your changes visually.

How am I feeling today?

Colour in how full your heart is and write out any emotions you are feeling today

Optimistic   *Hopeful*
Excited   *Thankful*

Next, check in with yourself and write down any emotions you are feeling. Acknowledging your feelings in this way helps you identify, accept and reduce the charge of any uncomfortable emotions. Instead of resisting, ignoring and pushing them aside, you are able to make peace with them and let them go so they do not continue to irritate you.

WHEEL OF EMOTIONS

This wheel of emotions, created by the Junto Institute, will help you pinpoint some of the emotions you might be feeling on any particular day.

Did you know there are a total of 34,000 emotions? Psychologist Robert Plutchik designed the original wheel of emotions, to help us to identify what emotion we are really feeling so that we can positively act on it.

Everything you write in this journal of yours is sacred to you. So always remember that no matter what you write about, no matter how big or small, your thoughts, words and emotions are all valid.

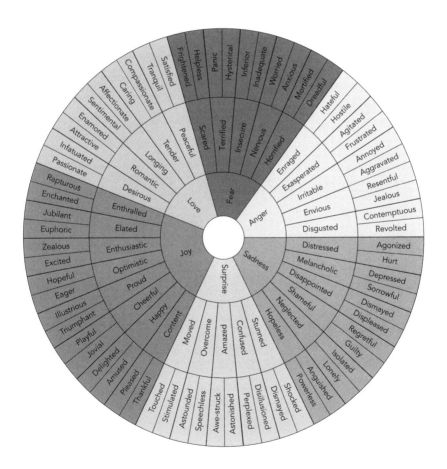

GRATITUDE IS THE ATTITUDE

In each entry, you will be asked two questions. The first will be a gratitude-led prompt that allows you to show appreciation and be more mindful of all the good in your life. The more gratitude we show, the more we receive to be grateful about. Writing down your blessings in life is a beautiful way to lift your mood.

SELF-REFLECTION

The second will be a self-reflection question that will make you dig a little deeper, think a little harder, and will help you reflect on your day. These questions will help you understand yourself a bit more, allow you to reflect on your actions and reactions, and encourage you to become more self-aware and mindful.

> What is one thing I am grateful for?
>
> *Having cuddles with my dog every morning*

> Who is someone I have not said 'I love you' to in a while?
>
> *My best friend, I should make more of an effort to tell her*

MIND, BODY, SPIRIT

Have you looked after your **mind**, **body** and **spirit** today? These simple tick boxes serve as a reminder to do something for yourself daily.

Looking after your mind, body and spirit helps you tune into your steady centre and remain balanced. As all three are interrelated, it is important to look after these areas of our lives and nurture our well-being on a conscious and deeper level.

If you wish, you can fill in this question at the end of the day. Choose whatever works best for you!

Have I taken care of my whole self today?

MIND

BODY

SPIRIT

Here are some examples to get you going:

MIND	BODY	SPIRIT

MIND

Engage in some mind puzzles

Read a book/article

Listen to a podcast

Watch a movie or documentary

Cook or bake

Attend a workshop or course

Listen to uplifting music

Have a digital detox

BODY

Do yoga asana, qigong or tai chi

Ensure you are getting quality sleep

Go for a swim, walk or hike

Eat nutritious food

Take a salt bath

Do some gardening

Take part in a breathwork session

Dance like no one is watching

SPIRIT

Meditate

Spend time in nature

Express gratitude

Connect with your friends

Volunteer or do an act of kindness

Laugh out loud

Practise forgiveness

Clear your space

Journaling

WRITE AND RELEASE

Last but not least, it is time to write and release anything that has been on your mind. This is a great way of releasing any emotions that do not serve you. Whether that is big, small, good or bad, this is your safe space to let it all out.

Write and release
Whatever is on your mind, write it out and let it go

My colleague dropped coffee on me and it embarassed me in front of my work friends. I know it wasn't their fault. I forgive them.

MY 30-DAY LIFE WHEEL

At the start of your journal and every thirty days thereafter, you will be filling in a life wheel diagram. This concept was originally created by Paul J. Meyer and is a fantastic visual tool to see how your life is balanced out and whether there are any areas you can improve on.

Here, you will be able to see and track your life as a whole, in one snapshot. This wheel has been split into ten different segments of your life. The key with filling this out is not to overthink and to go with the flow.

Once you have filled it in, have a think to see if you are giving too much or too little to any areas of your life. How does it make you feel? How can you do better? Use the space around the wheel to note ways in which you can add more balance to your life. This life wheel is something you can look back on and reflect on, and is a visual tool that will help you so much!

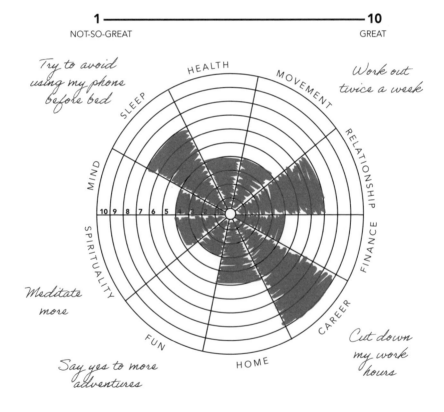

MINDFUL ACTIVITIES

Every three days, there will be an activity to do on the right-hand page. This provides an opportunity to get a little more creative, think deeper and mix things up!

These activity pages include 'worry jars', mindful techniques, small gratitude challenges, and everything in between. Every activity is set to benefit your well-being.

Always remember not to be too hard on yourself if you cannot commit to journaling that day. The beauty of this journal is that you can always go back to it whenever you like.

ROUTINE

How to create a positive daily structure that works for you

Routine serves as an anchor for our being and adds structure to our day, leaving us feeling more productive and focused. It helps us to create positive daily habits that we can achieve. Always start small and do not feel any pressure or need to do everything each morning or evening.

Do not be too hard on yourself if you are unable to stick to it every day. This is your routine, and it can be adapted to suit you. Your morning and evening routines allow you to prepare and wind down your mind, body and spirit for the day. Now it is time to establish your routines.

 ## MORNING ROUTINE

Ever heard the saying 'I woke up on the wrong side of the bed'? They say how you spend your morning sets the tone for the rest of your day. So, here are some things you can do to kickstart your day. The list below only contains suggestions, so find what works for you and do not try to implement too many at once. Feel free to switch things up to add excitement to your morning.

Skip the snooze button

Avoid looking at your phone first thing in the morning

Say a little affirmation or express gratitude

Visualize your day ahead

Make your bed

Do a short morning workout or some stretches to wake up your body

Shower and get yourself physically ready for the day

Take some time out to journal

Take a few minutes to meditate or do a guided meditation

Go for a morning walk and get some fresh air

Take your morning vitamins

Drink plenty of water

Listen to your favourite podcast or morning playlist

Make your morning drink or juice

Nurture your body with a nourishing breakfast

Check over your to-do list for the day

EVENING ROUTINE

Having an evening routine is just as important as having a morning routine. It helps us to unwind from our busy day and release any stress we may have built up throughout the day. Slowing down in the evening trains the brain to get itself into a calmer mindset and prepares the mind and body for sleep. Here are some practices that will help you feel lighter in the evening and prepare you for a good night's sleep:

Practise a short meditation or breathwork to calm the mind

Listen to a wellness podcast or audiobook

Read a book for twenty minutes

Enjoy a cup of herbal tea

Take your evening vitamins

Avoid screen time thirty minutes before bed

Take a relaxing bath or shower using aromatherapy products

Schedule ahead for the next day

Take the time to journal before sleeping

Go to bed at a reasonable time to get enough rest

EXAMPLE MORNING ROUTINE

Wake up and make the bed

Brush teeth and shower

Morning journaling

Hydrate and take vitamins

Go for a walk and listen to a mindful podcast

Nourishing breakfast

Check over to-do list

EXAMPLE EVENING ROUTINE

Have a herbal tea

Write tomorrow's to-do list

Avoid screen time

Evening meditation

Evening journaling

Brush teeth and get into bed

Read for fifteen minutes before sleeping

I MISSED A DAY

What to do when you fall behind

We can be our own worst critics at the best of times. It is OK to miss a day. To not be in the mood to journal. To fall off for a bit. Allow room for flexibility. Do not be too hard on yourself. Practise self-compassion. Listen to your needs and fulfil them.

Journaling is a transformative practice that is set to help you, not hurt you. So do not beat yourself up if you are unable to commit for a while. You are only human.

Just remember that if you ever take a step back, you still can step forward once again and resume your practice. This journal is not going anywhere and will always be here for you.

WHAT TO DO WHEN YOU MISS A DAY

Use your missed day as a day of rest

Do an extra page when you resume (if you like)

Do not beat yourself up about it – instead, look forward to what is ahead

Set an alarm every day for your dedicated journaling time

A PROMISE TO MYSELF

I _____ hereby agree that I will not be hard on myself if I miss a day's entry and will try my best to pick up where I left off.

Signed _____

Date _____

MY CALM KIT

Your toolbox for when things are feeling a bit too much

A Calm Kit is a great coping strategy to use whenever you are feeling low, anxious or overwhelmed. This is your go-to toolbox to pick yourself up again.

Simply write a list below (or even make a physical kit, if you wish) with all the things that help you feel better emotionally. Then, the next time you are going through a bad patch, feeling anxious, or feeling any sadness, all you have to do is come back to this list and pick an activity to help you feel more present, grounded and relaxed. This could be as simple as going for a walk.

(You can add to this list whenever you like.)

 MY CALM KIT

e.g. Listen to my favourite song

MY REVERSE
BUCKET LIST

A space to reflect on all of your accomplishments

It is easy to forget your accomplishments until you write them down and see them in front of you. When was the last time you looked back at all the things you have achieved in your life so far?

In this fast-paced world, we often remain busy with a plethora of daily tasks and future goals. Our minds constantly focus on what we need to do next or where we need to be. Rarely do we give ourselves the opportunity to look at how far we have come.

It is important to acknowledge your progress in both personal and professional life. Writing down your achievements is a simple yet effective way to remember how well you are doing despite your current circumstances. Each time you look at your list of accomplishments, you will experience a boost of happiness.

Try to set some time aside when you can and add them below, no matter how big or small they are. Not only will this give you a sense of gratitude for everything you have achieved and experienced, but any time you feel sadness or anxiety creeping in, this list can serve as a reminder that you have not only done beautiful things, but you are also capable of doing more.

(You do not need to fill it all out in one go.) Each time you look at your reverse bucket list, you will experience a boost of happiness.

MY REVERSE BUCKET LIST

e.g. I can ride a bicycle

MY JOURNAL

I CHOOSE TO BE HAPPY AND LOVE MYSELF

How am I feeling today?

Colour in how full your heart is and write out any emotions you are feeling today

_____   _____

_____   _____

No matter how big or small . . .

What is one thing I am grateful for?

_____

_____

_____

Who is someone I have not said 'I love you' to in a while?

_____

_____

_____

Have I taken care of my whole self today?

MIND ⬤

BODY ⬤

SPIRIT ⬤

Write and release

Whatever is on your mind, write it out and let it go

_____

_____

_____

_____

MY LIFE WHEEL

On a scale from 1 to 10, how am I feeling in the following areas of my life?
Do not overthink it, just colour it in!

1 ——————————————————————— **10**
NOT-SO-GREAT   GREAT

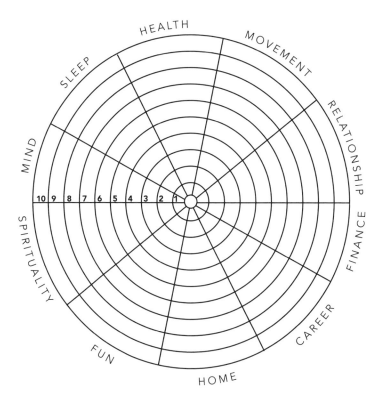

 Tip: *Use the space around the wheel to note ways in which you can add more balance to your life.*

ALL MY PROBLEMS HAVE SOLUTIONS

How am I feeling today?

Colour in how full your heart is and write out any emotions you are feeling today

_____   ♡   _____
_____   _____

No matter how big or small . . .

What is one good thing to always remember when I am feeling low?

_____

_____

_____

How can I show myself more compassion?

_____

_____

_____

Have I taken care of my whole self today?

MIND ⬤

BODY ⬤

SPIRIT ⬤

Write and release

Whatever is on your mind, write it out and let it go

_____

_____

_____

_____

I AM A MAGNET FOR POSITIVITY AND BLESSINGS

How am I feeling today?

Colour in how full your heart is and write out any emotions you are feeling today

$\heartsuit$

_____ _____

_____ _____

No matter how big or small . . .

My greatest strength is . . .

_____

_____

_____

What is a scent that brings back good memories?

_____

_____

_____

Have I taken care of my whole self today?	Write and release
	Whatever is on your mind, write it out and let it go
MIND ⚪	
BODY ⚪	
SPIRIT ⚪	

I RELEASE THE PAST, STEP INTO THE PRESENT, AND LOOK FORWARD TO THE FUTURE

How am I feeling today?

Colour in how full your heart is and write out any emotions you are feeling today

_____   ♡   _____

No matter how big or small . . .

I feel happiest when . . .

_____

_____

_____

What excites me most about my future?

_____

_____

_____

Have I taken care of my whole self today?

MIND ●

BODY ●

SPIRIT ●

Write and release

Whatever is on your mind, write it out and let it go

_____

_____

_____

_____

WRITE A LETTER TO YOUR FUTURE SELF

 Write yourself a letter to read later. How do you see yourself and your life in the future? Visualize what it looks like and describe it in your letter. For example, 'I am proud of how far you have come with your career and how confident you are.' Be specific, be positive, and let things flow.

Dear future self,

I WELCOME ALL FORMS OF LOVE INTO MY LIFE

How am I feeling today?

Colour in how full your heart is and write out any emotions you are feeling today

_____   _____

_____   _____

No matter how big or small . . .

Someone or something that gives me a feeling of comfort is . . .

_____

_____

_____

What is something I take for granted?

_____

_____

_____

Have I taken care of my whole self today?

MIND

BODY

SPIRIT

Write and release

Whatever is on your mind, write it out and let it go

_____

_____

_____

_____

I WHOLEHEARTEDLY LOVE MYSELF TODAY

How am I feeling today?

Colour in how full your heart is and write out any emotions you are feeling today

_____   _____

_____   _____

No matter how big or small . . .

My favourite self-care act is . . .

_____

_____

_____

What is something I want to focus on tomorrow?

_____

_____

_____

Have I taken
care of my
whole self
today?

Write and release

Whatever is on your mind, write it out and let it go

MIND

BODY

SPIRIT

I EMBRACE MYSELF AND THE PRESENT MOMENT

How am I feeling today?

Colour in how full your heart is and write out any emotions you are feeling today

_____   _____

_____   _____

No matter how big or small . . .

What makes me feel loved?

_____

_____

_____

My perfect morning looks like . . .

_____

_____

_____

Have I taken care of my whole self today?

MIND

BODY

SPIRIT

Write and release

Whatever is on your mind, write it out and let it go

_____

_____

_____

_____

GROUNDING

Sometimes we can forget the beauty of being in the 'now'. Doing regular grounding exercises can help you feel calm and help your mind stay more focused on the present, rather than looking to the past or future.

5 THINGS I CAN SEE

4 THINGS I CAN FEEL

3 THINGS I CAN HEAR

2 THINGS I CAN SMELL

1 THING I CAN TASTE

Tip: *Try this exercise whenever you are feeling overwhelmed.*

I CELEBRATE MY WINS – BIG OR SMALL

How am I feeling today?

Colour in how full your heart is and write out any emotions you are feeling today

_____   ♡   _____

_____   _____

No matter how big or small . . .

What is one thing that brings me joy?

_____

_____

_____

What is a new skill I want to learn?

_____

_____

_____

Have I taken care of my whole self today?

MIND ●

BODY ●

SPIRIT ●

Write and release

Whatever is on your mind, write it out and let it go

_____

_____

_____

_____

I WILL KEEP AN OPEN MIND THAT IS FREE FROM JUDGEMENT

How am I feeling today?

Colour in how full your heart is and write out any emotions you are feeling today

_____ ♡ _____
_____   _____

No matter how big or small . . .

I am looking forward to . . .

_____
_____
_____

How do I enjoy spending my free time?

_____
_____
_____

Have I taken care of my whole self today?

MIND

BODY

SPIRIT

Write and release

Whatever is on your mind, write it out and let it go

_____
_____
_____
_____

I RAISE MY VIBRATION WITH EVERY BREATH I TAKE

How am I feeling today?

Colour in how full your heart is and write out any emotions you are feeling today

_____

_____

_____

_____

No matter how big or small . . .

I feel most content when . . .

_____

_____

_____

What is one thing I can do to reduce stress in my life?

_____

_____

_____

Have I taken care of my whole self today?

MIND ●

BODY ●

SPIRIT ●

Write and release

Whatever is on your mind, write it out and let it go

_____

_____

_____

_____

BOX BREATHING

Our breath is one thing that changes with every emotion. You may breathe faster when you are worried or skip a few breaths when you are excited. We may not be able to control our emotions at times, but we can take control of our breathing, which, in return, can help us feel a sense of calm.

Repeat this small box breathing exercise daily if you can, or whenever you feel you need it.

 Tip: Feel free to add this to your Calm Kit (page 22).

I AM THRIVING. I AM FLOURISHING. I AM BLOOMING.

How am I feeling today?

Colour in how full your heart is and write out any emotions you are feeling today

_____   ♡   _____
_____   _____

No matter how big or small . . .

A place I am grateful for is . . .

_____

_____

_____

What place do I want to visit the most and why?

_____

_____

_____

Have I taken
care of my
whole self
today?

MIND ●

BODY ●

SPIRIT ●

Write and release
Whatever is on your mind, write it out and let it go

_____

_____

_____

_____

THE LOVE THAT I GIVE TO OTHERS DOES NOT GO UNNOTICED

How am I feeling today?

Colour in how full your heart is and write out any emotions you are feeling today

_____

_____

_____

_____

No matter how big or small . . .

What makes me feel worthy?

_____

_____

_____

How present do I feel today?

_____

_____

_____

Have I taken care of my whole self today?

MIND

BODY

SPIRIT

Write and release

Whatever is on your mind, write it out and let it go

_____

_____

_____

_____

I LET GO OF NEGATIVE THOUGHTS THAT DO NOT SERVE ME

How am I feeling today?

Colour in how full your heart is and write out any emotions you are feeling today

_____   ♡   _____
_____   _____

No matter how big or small . . .

What is one reason to smile?

_____

_____

_____

One breakdown in my life that led me to a breakthrough is . . .

_____

_____

_____

Have I taken
care of my
whole self
today?

MIND ●

BODY ●

SPIRIT ●

Write and release

Whatever is on your mind, write it out and let it go

_____

_____

_____

_____

WORRY JAR

Firstly, it is OK to worry. Writing these worries out on paper is a great way of releasing any heavy emotions that they bring. No matter how big or small, fill the jar below with any worries you have. The last step is to draw a lid onto your worry jar to lock them away.

 Tip: *Next time you have an empty jar, make it into a physical worry jar!*

I AM GREATER THAN THE PERSON I WAS YESTERDAY

How am I feeling today?

Colour in how full your heart is and write out any emotions you are feeling today

_____   _____

_____   ♡   _____

No matter how big or small . . .

What is one of the best things about being me?

_____

_____

_____

If love were a colour, what would it be and why?

_____

_____

_____

Have I taken care of my whole self today?

MIND ◯

BODY ◯

SPIRIT ◯

Write and release

Whatever is on your mind, write it out and let it go

_____

_____

_____

_____

I RECOGNIZE MY OWN TALENTS AND GIFTS

How am I feeling today?

Colour in how full your heart is and write out any emotions you are feeling today

_____ ♡ _____
_____   _____

No matter how big or small . . .

How does being out in nature make me feel?

_____

_____

_____

What is something I could talk about for hours?

_____

_____

_____

Have I taken care of my whole self today?

MIND ⬤

BODY ⬤

SPIRIT ⬤

Write and release

Whatever is on your mind, write it out and let it go

_____

_____

_____

_____

I BREATHE IN CONFIDENCE AND EXHALE FEAR

How am I feeling today?

Colour in how full your heart is and write out any emotions you are feeling today

_____   ♡   _____
_____   _____

No matter how big or small . . .

What is one thing I am proud of?

_____

_____

_____

The best advice I have ever received is . . .

_____

_____

_____

Have I taken care of my whole self today?

MIND ●

BODY ●

SPIRIT ●

Write and release

Whatever is on your mind, write it out and let it go

_____

_____

_____

_____

YOUR SPACE TO EXPRESS YOURSELF

Use this page to jot down thoughts, to-do lists, doodles – anything your heart or mind desires. This is your story to tell.

I HAVE THE POWER TO CREATE CHANGE

How am I feeling today?

Colour in how full your heart is and write out any emotions you are feeling today

_____   _____

_____   _____

No matter how big or small . . .

A quality that I admire in someone I love is . . .

_____

_____

_____

Loving myself means . . .

_____

_____

_____

Have I taken care of my whole self today?

MIND 🔘

BODY 🔘

SPIRIT 🔘

Write and release

Whatever is on your mind, write it out and let it go

_____

_____

_____

_____

I AM EXACTLY WHERE I AM MEANT TO BE

How am I feeling today?

Colour in how full your heart is and write out any emotions you are feeling today

_____   ♡   _____
_____   _____

No matter how big or small . . .

The best gift I have ever received is . . .

_____

_____

_____

The best gift I have ever given is . . .

_____

_____

_____

Have I taken
care of my
whole self
today?

Write and release

Whatever is on your mind, write it out and let it go

MIND ●

BODY ●

SPIRIT ●

_____

_____

_____

_____

I HAVE LOVE IN MY HEART AND SHARE IT WITH THE WORLD AROUND ME

How am I feeling today?

Colour in how full your heart is and write out any emotions you are feeling today

_____   _____

_____   _____

No matter how big or small . . .

Who is someone I can send a message of gratitude to and why?

_____

_____

_____

What is the best piece of advice I have ever given to someone?

_____

_____

_____

Have I taken care of my whole self today?

MIND

BODY

SPIRIT

Write and release

Whatever is on your mind, write it out and let it go

_____

_____

_____

_____

GRATITUDE CHALLENGE

 Challenge yourself to have a great day. Tick any of the below that you have managed to do recently. (One is left blank for you to fill in with something that is personal to you.)

LISTEN TO A GUIDED GRATITUDE MEDITATION

COUNT YOUR BLESSINGS

LEAVE A NICE REVIEW FOR A LOCAL COMPANY

THANK SOMEONE WHO HAS HELPED YOU

CHECK IN WITH A LOVED ONE

JOURNAL YOUR THOUGHTS

I RELEASE NEGATIVE SELF-TALK ABOUT MYSELF AND OTHERS

How am I feeling today?

Colour in how full your heart is and write out any emotions you are feeling today

_____   _____
_____   _____

No matter how big or small . . .

Someone I look up to is . . .

_____

_____

_____

I am going to be gentle on myself because . . .

_____

_____

_____

Have I taken care of my whole self today?

MIND ⬤

BODY ⬤

SPIRIT ⬤

Write and release

Whatever is on your mind, write it out and let it go

_____

_____

_____

_____

TODAY I CHOOSE TO BE KIND, LOVING AND CARING

How am I feeling today?

Colour in how full your heart is and write out any emotions you are feeling today

_____   _____

_____   _____

No matter how big or small . . .

I can be kind to myself by . . .

_____

_____

_____

My inner child needs to hear . . .

_____

_____

_____

Have I taken care of my whole self today?

MIND

BODY

SPIRIT

Write and release

Whatever is on your mind, write it out and let it go

_____

_____

_____

_____

HAPPINESS IS ALWAYS AVAILABLE TO ME

How am I feeling today?

Colour in how full your heart is and write out any emotions you are feeling today

_____   _____

No matter how big or small . . .

I am grateful that I live in a world where . . .

_____

_____

_____

What would I like to dream about tonight?

_____

_____

_____

Have I taken care of my whole self today?

MIND

BODY

SPIRIT

Write and release

Whatever is on your mind, write it out and let it go

_____

_____

_____

_____

MY HAPPY PLACE

Think of a place where you feel your happiest.

What does it look like? What are you wearing? What can you hear? What can you feel? Is anyone with you? Draw a picture or stick a photo of this place in the space below and write what your five senses can feel around the image. For example, 'It is warm and sunny.' Be as specific as you like.

Whenever you are feeling down, take a moment to focus on your breath and meditate on your happy place.

 Tip: *Add your happy place to your Calm Kit (page 22).*

I AM PATIENT AND KIND TO MYSELF AS I HEAL

How am I feeling today?

Colour in how full your heart is and write out any emotions you are feeling today

_____   ♡   _____

_____   _____

No matter how big or small . . .

A happy moment I recently experienced is . . .

_____

_____

_____

I know I am healing when . . .

_____

_____

_____

Have I taken care of my whole self today?

MIND ⬤

BODY ⬤

SPIRIT ⬤

Write and release

Whatever is on your mind, write it out and let it go

_____

_____

_____

_____

MY LIFE IS FULL OF ENDLESS JOY AND BLESSINGS

How am I feeling today?

Colour in how full your heart is and write out any emotions you are feeling today

_____   ♡   _____
_____   _____

No matter how big or small . . .

What are the things I currently love and accept about myself?

_____
_____
_____

Who do I rely on the most for assistance/help and why?

_____
_____
_____

Have I taken care of my whole self today?

MIND

BODY

SPIRIT

Write and release

Whatever is on your mind, write it out and let it go

_____
_____
_____
_____

I LOVE AND RESPECT MYSELF UNCONDITIONALLY

How am I feeling today?

Colour in how full your heart is and write out any emotions you are feeling today

_____   _____

_____   _____

No matter how big or small . . .

What are three things I value about my body?

_____

_____

_____

I describe my personality as . . .

_____

_____

_____

Have I taken care of my whole self today?

MIND

BODY

SPIRIT

Write and release

Whatever is on your mind, write it out and let it go

_____

_____

_____

_____

AFFIRM IT

Affirming positive thoughts can have transformative effects. Write out and repeat the affirmation below.

I AM WORTHY OF LOVE

I AM LETTING GO OF ALL SHAME AND GUILT

How am I feeling today?

Colour in how full your heart is and write out any emotions you are feeling today

_____   _____

No matter how big or small . . .

What memory will I hold on to for ever?

_____

_____

_____

When I make a mistake, how do I forgive myself?

_____

_____

_____

Have I taken care of my whole self today?

MIND

BODY

SPIRIT

Write and release

Whatever is on your mind, write it out and let it go

_____

_____

_____

_____

I INHALE STRENGTH AND EXHALE WEAKNESS

How am I feeling today?

Colour in how full your heart is and write out any emotions you are feeling today

_____ _____

No matter how big or small . . .

What is the most comforting thing someone has ever said to me?

_____

_____

_____

How do I regain control of my nerves in a stressful situation?

_____

_____

_____

Have I taken
care of my
whole self
today?

MIND

BODY

SPIRIT

Write and release

Whatever is on your mind, write it out and let it go

_____

_____

_____

_____

MY MIND IS AT PEACE DESPITE WHAT IS HAPPENING AROUND ME

How am I feeling today?

Colour in how full your heart is and write out any emotions you are feeling today

_____   _____

_____   _____

No matter how big or small . . .

What is one beautiful reason to be happy right now?

_____

_____

_____

Is there anything I would like more of in my life?

_____

_____

_____

Have I taken care of my whole self today?

MIND

BODY

SPIRIT

Write and release

Whatever is on your mind, write it out and let it go

_____

_____

_____

_____

MINDFUL COLOURING

Colouring is a great way to get into a meditative state by calming the mind and feeling relaxed. Let your creativity flow and colour the below.

I AM MY LONGEST COMMITMENT AND THEREFORE CARE FOR MYSELF DEEPLY

How am I feeling today?

Colour in how full your heart is and write out any emotions you are feeling today

No matter how big or small . . .

What is something that I am proud of doing for myself recently?

How can I prioritize myself without feeling guilty?

Have I taken care of my whole self today?

MIND

BODY

SPIRIT

Write and release

Whatever is on your mind, write it out and let it go

I GIVE MYSELF PERMISSION TO SLOW DOWN

How am I feeling today?

Colour in how full your heart is and write out any emotions you are feeling today

_____   ♡   _____

No matter how big or small . . .

What is something someone has done for me that I am thankful for?

_____

_____

In moments of stress, what can I do to be more present?

_____

_____

Have I taken care of my whole self today?

MIND

BODY

SPIRIT

Write and release

Whatever is on your mind, write it out and let it go

_____

_____

_____

_____

MY DESIRES ARE MANIFESTING AT A RAPID RATE

How am I feeling today?

Colour in how full your heart is and write out any emotions you are feeling today

_____

_____

_____

_____

No matter how big or small . . .

Who is one person (past or present) I am grateful for in my life?

_____

_____

_____

What is one area of my life I would like to improve on?

_____

_____

_____

Have I taken care of my whole self today?

MIND ⬤

BODY ⬤

SPIRIT ⬤

Write and release

Whatever is on your mind, write it out and let it go

_____

_____

_____

_____

MY LIFE WHEEL

On a scale from 1 to 10, how am I feeling in the following areas of my life? Do not overthink it, just colour it in!

1 ———————————————————————— **10**

NOT-SO-GREAT   GREAT

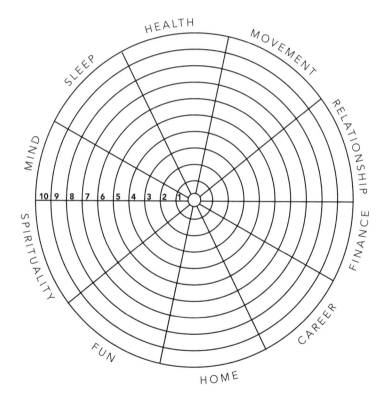

 Tip: *Use the space around the wheel to note ways in which you can add more balance to your life.*

SOMETHING WONDERFUL IS ABOUT TO HAPPEN TO ME

How am I feeling today?
Colour in how full your heart is and write out any emotions you are feeling today

_____ ♡ _____

_____   _____

No matter how big or small . . .

I know I am happy when . . .

_____

_____

_____

What is a goal I would like to achieve and why?

_____

_____

_____

Have I taken care of my whole self today?

MIND ●

BODY ●

SPIRIT ●

Write and release
Whatever is on your mind, write it out and let it go

_____

_____

_____

_____

OPPORTUNITIES ARE ALL AROUND ME

How am I feeling today?

Colour in how full your heart is and write out any emotions you are feeling today

_____   _____

_____   _____

No matter how big or small . . .

I could not imagine my life without . . .

_____

_____

_____

Who or what motivates me and why?

_____

_____

_____

Have I taken care of my whole self today?

MIND

BODY

SPIRIT

Write and release

Whatever is on your mind, write it out and let it go

_____

_____

_____

_____

I CONTINUE TO FOCUS ON WHAT I WANT TO ATTRACT INTO MY LIFE

How am I feeling today?

Colour in how full your heart is and write out any emotions you are feeling today

_____

_____

_____

_____

No matter how big or small . . .

Who is someone that is nice to me?

_____

_____

Is there anything missing in my life?

_____

_____

Have I taken care of my whole self today?	Write and release
	Whatever is on your mind, write it out and let it go
MIND ●	_____
BODY ●	_____
SPIRIT ●	_____
	_____

WORDSEARCH

Take some time away from your digital device and search for some empowering words!

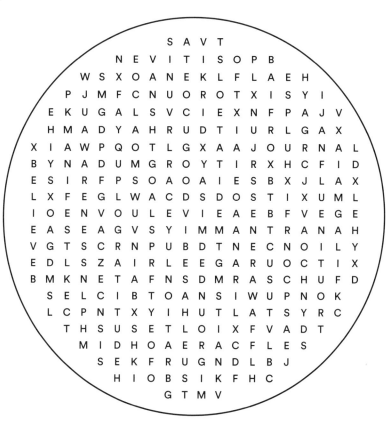

CRYSTAL	AWARENESS	CLEANSE	GRATITUDE	HEAL
GOALS	COURAGE	MANIFEST	MANTRA	VIBRATION
SELF CARE	GROUNDED	POSITIVE	BELIEVE	GOOD VIBES
MEDITATE	YOGA	ROUTINE	JOURNAL	RISE

I AM COMMITTED TO MY PATH AND WHOLEHEARTEDLY BELIEVE IN MYSELF

How am I feeling today?

Colour in how full your heart is and write out any emotions you are feeling today

_____   ♡   _____
_____   _____

No matter how big or small . . .

What is most important to me right now?

_____

_____

_____

What prevents me from taking the next steps in work, life or experiences?

_____

_____

_____

Have I taken care of my whole self today?

MIND ◐

BODY ◐

SPIRIT ◐

Write and release

Whatever is on your mind, write it out and let it go

_____

_____

_____

_____

MY ENERGY IS POSITIVE, PURE AND POWERFUL

How am I feeling today?

Colour in how full your heart is and write out any emotions you are feeling today

_____   ♡   _____

No matter how big or small . . .

Who is that one person that I will protect forever?

_____

_____

_____

What is one change I can make that is more aligned with my values?

_____

_____

_____

Have I taken care of my whole self today?

MIND ○

BODY ○

SPIRIT ○

Write and release

Whatever is on your mind, write it out and let it go

_____

_____

_____

_____

I AM FOCUSED, GROUNDED AND PEACEFUL

How am I feeling today?

Colour in how full your heart is and write out any emotions you are feeling today

_____   _____

_____   _____

No matter how big or small . . .

Who is someone that makes me feel grounded?

_____

_____

_____

When do I feel most connected to myself?

_____

_____

_____

Have I taken
care of my
whole self
today?

MIND ●

BODY ●

SPIRIT ●

Write and release

Whatever is on your mind, write it out and let it go

_____

_____

_____

_____

MY SPIRIT SIGN

 Have you ever looked a little deeper into your star sign? We have more than one star sign. Our spirit sign consists of our sun sign (also known as our star sign), moon sign and rising sun that can make us who we are. Spend a few moments and research on the internet to find out your sun, moon and rising sun sign.

☼ SUN SIGN

Rules your personality and how you behave most of the time

☾ MOON SIGN

Rules your emotional core and determines your mood

☀ RISING SUN

Rules your outer appearance and how others see you

I AM CREATING A LIFE I LOVE

How am I feeling today?

Colour in how full your heart is and write out any emotions you are feeling today

_____   ♡   _____
_____   _____

No matter how big or small . . .

Who is one person or what is one thing I love today?

_____
_____
_____

How can I respond better in situations, rather than reacting in them?

_____
_____
_____

Have I taken care of my whole self today?

MIND ⬤

BODY ⬤

SPIRIT ⬤

Write and release
Whatever is on your mind, write it out and let it go

_____
_____
_____
_____

THE LIGHT I SEEK IS WITHIN ME

How am I feeling today?

Colour in how full your heart is and write out any emotions you are feeling today

_____   ♡   _____
_____   _____

No matter how big or small . . .

What is one constant in my life and how does it make me feel?

_____

_____

_____

Is there a boundary I need to set in my life?

_____

_____

_____

Have I taken
care of my
whole self
today?

MIND ⬤

BODY ⬤

SPIRIT ⬤

Write and release

Whatever is on your mind, write it out and let it go

_____

_____

_____

_____

I AM DIVINE. I AM WHOLE. I AM ENOUGH.

How am I feeling today?

Colour in how full your heart is and write out any emotions you are feeling today

_____   _____

_____   _____

No matter how big or small . . .

What is one compliment I can give myself right now?

_____

_____

_____

Dear Universe . . .

_____

_____

_____

Have I taken care of my whole self today?	Write and release
	Whatever is on your mind, write it out and let it go
MIND ●	_____
BODY ●	_____
SPIRIT ●	_____
	_____

COLOURING QUOTE

 Colouring is a great way to get into a meditative state by calming the mind and feeling relaxed. Visualize and feel the words below as you colour.

No one is me and that is my power

MY INTENTIONS ARE SUPPORTED AND SERVE MY HIGHER SELF

How am I feeling today?

Colour in how full your heart is and write out any emotions you are feeling today

_____   _____

_____   _____

No matter how big or small . . .

A goal I have recently achieved is . . .

_____

_____

_____

What is my biggest weakness?

_____

_____

_____

Have I taken care of my whole self today?

MIND

BODY

SPIRIT

Write and release

Whatever is on your mind, write it out and let it go

_____

_____

_____

_____

I NURTURE INNER PEACE BY LOVING ALL PARTS OF ME

How am I feeling today?

Colour in how full your heart is and write out any emotions you are feeling today

_____   _____

No matter how big or small . . .

What are three things I value in myself?

What are three things I value in others?

Have I taken care of my whole self today?

MIND

BODY

SPIRIT

Write and release

Whatever is on your mind, write it out and let it go

I MAKE TIME TO CARE FOR MYSELF AND MEET MY NEEDS

How am I feeling today?

Colour in how full your heart is and write out any emotions you are feeling today

_____

_____   _____

_____

No matter how big or small . . .

How can I show myself love each day?

_____

_____

_____

How can I add more fun to my day?

_____

_____

_____

Have I taken care of my whole self today?

MIND

BODY

SPIRIT

Write and release

Whatever is on your mind, write it out and let it go

_____

_____

_____

_____

SELF-CARE BINGO

 Can you complete a row, column or diagonal in a different kind of bingo? Up your self-care game and give yourself some TLC.

YOU DESERVE THE BEST THINGS

DO YOUR SKINCARE	BE IN NATURE	HAVE YOUR FAVE DRINK	UNPLUG	LISTEN TO MUSIC
HYDRATE	READ	BURN A CANDLE	WATCH YOUR FAVE MOVIE	SMILE
8 HOURS OF SLEEP	PAINTING	BAKING	JOURNAL	TRY SOMETHING NEW
MOVE YOUR BODY	CUDDLE A PET OR HUMAN	ME TIME	BUBBLE BATH	TAKE A NAP
PRACTISE A HOBBY	MEET UP WITH FRIENDS	MEDITATE	COLOUR	DANCE

I EFFORTLESSLY ATTRACT ALL THAT I WANT AND ALL THAT I NEED

How am I feeling today?

Colour in how full your heart is and write out any emotions you are feeling today

_____

_____   _____

_____

No matter how big or small . . .

What is one thing I have today that I dreamt of having in the past?

_____

_____

_____

Is there anything that scares me?

_____

_____

_____

Have I taken care of my whole self today?

Write and release

Whatever is on your mind, write it out and let it go

_____

MIND

_____

BODY

_____

SPIRIT

_____

I BELIEVE IN WHAT I AM BEING GUIDED TOWARDS

How am I feeling today?

Colour in how full your heart is and write out any emotions you are feeling today

_____   ♡   _____

_____   _____

No matter how big or small . . .

Which past experience am I most thankful for and why?

_____

_____

_____

Is there anything I need to work on to better myself?

_____

_____

_____

Have I taken care of my whole self today?

MIND ●

BODY ●

SPIRIT ●

Write and release

Whatever is on your mind, write it out and let it go

_____

_____

_____

_____

I RADIATE LOVE, CONFIDENCE AND POSITIVITY

How am I feeling today?

Colour in how full your heart is and write out any emotions you are feeling today

_____   ♡   _____
_____   _____

No matter how big or small . . .

Who is someone I am deeply grateful for?

_____

_____

_____

When was the last time I did something out of my comfort zone?

_____

_____

_____

Have I taken
care of my
whole self
today?

MIND ●

BODY ●

SPIRIT ●

Write and release

Whatever is on your mind, write it out and let it go

_____

_____

_____

_____

WOULD YOU RATHER . . . ?

 Doing this activity will help you explore what you like and who you are. From the choices below, tick the activity you would prefer to do.

GO ON
A WALK
**GO FOR
A RUN**

CALL A
FRIEND
**TEXT A
FRIEND**

LISTEN TO
MUSIC
**LISTEN TO A
PODCAST**

SPEND TIME
ALONE
**SPEND TIME
WITH OTHERS**

HAVE AN
EARLY NIGHT IN
**HAVE A LATE
NIGHT OUT**

GUIDED
MEDITATION
**NON-GUIDED
MEDITATION**

DO YOGA
ASANA
**SIT IN
MEDITATION**

RELIVE THE
PAST
**KNOW YOUR
FUTURE**

GO ON A
BEACH BREAK
**GO ON A
CITY BREAK**

READ A
BOOK
**WATCH A
MOVIE**

BE ABLE TO
READ MINDS
**COMMUNICATE
WITH ANIMALS**

JOURNAL IN
THE MORNING
**JOURNAL IN
THE EVENING**

I ATTRACT LOVING AND POSITIVE PEOPLE INTO MY LIFE

How am I feeling today?

Colour in how full your heart is and write out any emotions you are feeling today

_____   ♡   _____

_____   _____

No matter how big or small . . .

Who is someone that has supported me to get to where I am today?

_____

_____

_____

What is a relationship I need to let go of?

_____

_____

_____

Have I taken care of my whole self today?

MIND ●

BODY ●

SPIRIT ●

Write and release

Whatever is on your mind, write it out and let it go

_____

_____

_____

_____

MY STRENGTH IS IN MY COMPASSION FOR ALL BEINGS

How am I feeling today?

Colour in how full your heart is and write out any emotions you are feeling today

No matter how big or small . . .

I feel most at peace when . . .

_____

_____

_____

What needs of mine have not been met yet?

_____

_____

_____

Have I taken care of my whole self today?

MIND

BODY

SPIRIT

Write and release

Whatever is on your mind, write it out and let it go

_____

_____

_____

_____

I INVITE GRATITUDE INTO MY HEART AND MIND

How am I feeling today?

Colour in how full your heart is and write out any emotions you are feeling today

_____   ♡   _____
_____   _____

No matter how big or small . . .

What is a compliment I have received that made me feel special?

_____

_____

_____

Is there something I could do today to make tomorrow easier?

_____

_____

_____

Have I taken care of my whole self today?

MIND ●

BODY ●

SPIRIT ●

Write and release

Whatever is on your mind, write it out and let it go

_____

_____

_____

_____

SELF-LOVE CHALLENGE

 Challenge yourself to have some extra self-love today. Tick any of the below that you have managed to do recently. (One is left blank for you to fill in with something that is personal to you.)

SAY THREE
THINGS YOU LIKE
ABOUT YOURSELF

TAKE SOME TIME
OUT FOR
YOURSELF

MAKE YOURSELF A HOT DRINK

DO SOMETHING
THAT BRINGS
YOU JOY

LISTEN TO YOUR
FAVOURITE
SONG

RUN A RELAXING
SALT BATH

MY VIBRATION IS ALIGNED TO ABUNDANCE AND PROSPERITY

How am I feeling today?

Colour in how full your heart is and write out any emotions you are feeling today

_____ ♡ _____

_____   _____

No matter how big or small . . .

Something that keeps me hopeful is . . .

_____

_____

_____

Where does my inner child exist in my body?

_____

_____

_____

Have I taken care of my whole self today?

MIND ⬤

BODY ⬤

SPIRIT ⬤

Write and release

Whatever is on your mind, write it out and let it go

_____

_____

_____

_____

MY ENERGY IS VIBRANT AND UPLIFTS OTHERS

How am I feeling today?

Colour in how full your heart is and write out any emotions you are feeling today

_____   ♡   _____
_____   _____

No matter how big or small . . .

What am I doing this year to make myself happy?

_____

_____

_____

What is something I wish someone would ask me?

_____

_____

_____

Have I taken
care of my
whole self
today?

MIND ◯

BODY ◯

SPIRIT ◯

Write and release

Whatever is on your mind, write it out and let it go

_____

_____

_____

_____

I AM CREATING THE LIFE OF MY DREAMS

How am I feeling today?

Colour in how full your heart is and write out any emotions you are feeling today

_____   _____
_____   _____

No matter how big or small . . .

Who is one person that has given me support on a bad day?

_____

_____

_____

What is one thing I would be good at but have never tried?

_____

_____

_____

Have I taken care of my whole self today?

MIND

BODY

SPIRIT

Write and release

Whatever is on your mind, write it out and let it go

_____

_____

_____

_____

MY BUCKET LIST

What are some of your dreams and aspirations? When you write your goals down, you turn your intentions into something tangible which forces clarity and creates a deeper connection to them. It is time to make your bucket list!

-
-
-
-
-
-
-
-
-
-
-
-
-
-
-
-
-
-

I AM WRAPPED IN THE LOVING ENERGY OF THE UNIVERSE

How am I feeling today?

Colour in how full your heart is and write out any emotions you are feeling today

_____

_____

_____

_____

No matter how big or small . . .

Someone who inspires me to be the best version of myself is . . .

_____

_____

_____

I wish I had more time for . . .

_____

_____

_____

Have I taken care of my whole self today?

MIND

BODY

SPIRIT

Write and release

Whatever is on your mind, write it out and let it go

_____

_____

_____

_____

I AM UNAPOLOGETICALLY MY AUTHENTIC SELF

How am I feeling today?

Colour in how full your heart is and write out any emotions you are feeling today

_____   _____

No matter how big or small . . .

Something I hope to never forget is . . .

_____

_____

_____

What areas of my life have I been avoiding and why?

_____

_____

_____

Have I taken care of my whole self today?

MIND

BODY

SPIRIT

Write and release

Whatever is on your mind, write it out and let it go

_____

_____

_____

_____

I HAVE THE POWER I NEED TO BE THE BEST VERSION OF MYSELF

How am I feeling today?

Colour in how full your heart is and write out any emotions you are feeling today

_____   _____
_____   _____

No matter how big or small . . .

Who is my best friend and why?

_____

_____

_____

What is one superpower I would want and why?

_____

_____

_____

Have I taken care of my whole self today?

MIND

BODY

SPIRIT

Write and release

Whatever is on your mind, write it out and let it go

_____

_____

_____

_____

PRESENT ME VS FUTURE ME

Where do you see yourself in the future? Use the columns below to write out where you are in the present moment in life and where you would like to see yourself in the future. Dream big!

PRESENT

e.g. Hitting 5k steps a day

FUTURE

e.g. Walking 10k steps a day

 Tip: *Create a vision board from your future list.*

TODAY IS FULL OF BLESSINGS, MIRACLES AND OPPORTUNITIES

How am I feeling today?

Colour in how full your heart is and write out any emotions you are feeling today

_____

_____

_____

_____

No matter how big or small . . .

Who is someone that helped me through a difficult time?

_____

_____

_____

How do I reward myself?

_____

_____

_____

Have I taken care of my whole self today?

MIND

BODY

SPIRIT

Write and release

Whatever is on your mind, write it out and let it go

_____

_____

_____

_____

I RELEASE SELF-JUDGEMENT AND EMBRACE SELF-WORTH

How am I feeling today?

Colour in how full your heart is and write out any emotions you are feeling today

_____   _____

_____   _____

No matter how big or small . . .

Loving myself looks like . . .

_____

_____

_____

I know I am hurting when . . .

_____

_____

_____

Have I taken care of my whole self today?

MIND ◯

BODY ◯

SPIRIT ◯

Write and release

Whatever is on your mind, write it out and let it go

_____

_____

_____

_____

I AM FULFILLING MY PURPOSE

How am I feeling today?

Colour in how full your heart is and write out any emotions you are feeling today

_____   _____

_____   _____

No matter how big or small . . .

What was the last thing that really made me laugh?

_____

_____

_____

What is one choice I can make that not everyone gets to make?

_____

_____

_____

Have I taken care of my whole self today?

MIND

BODY

SPIRIT

Write and release

Whatever is on your mind, write it out and let it go

_____

_____

_____

_____

I . . .

Finish the sentence with as little or as much as you wish.

I AM

I FEEL

I WISH

I THINK

I CREATE

I LOVE

I TRUST THAT I AM ON THE RIGHT PATH

How am I feeling today?

Colour in how full your heart is and write out any emotions you are feeling today

No matter how big or small . . .

Who plays the biggest role in my life?

I know I am not my thoughts because . . .

Have I taken care of my whole self today?

MIND

BODY

SPIRIT

Write and release

Whatever is on your mind, write it out and let it go

I AM GRATEFUL FOR ALL THE LITTLE JOYS IN MY LIFE

How am I feeling today?

Colour in how full your heart is and write out any emotions you are feeling today

_____

_____

No matter how big or small . . .

The last good deed I did was . . .

_____

_____

_____

What compliment would I give to my past self?

_____

_____

_____

Have I taken care of my whole self today?

MIND

BODY

SPIRIT

Write and release

Whatever is on your mind, write it out and let it go

_____

_____

_____

_____

I LOVE WHO I AM BECOMING

How am I feeling today?

Colour in how full your heart is and write out any emotions you are feeling today

_____   ♡   _____
_____   _____

No matter how big or small . . .

Someone who believes in me is . . .

_____

_____

_____

What is one way I can make a difference in someone's life tomorrow?

_____

_____

_____

Have I taken
care of my
whole self
today?

MIND ●

BODY ●

SPIRIT ●

Write and release

Whatever is on your mind, write it out and let it go

_____

_____

_____

_____

MY LIFE WHEEL

On a scale from 1 to 10, how am I feeling in the following areas of my life?
Do not overthink it, just colour it in!

1 ——————————————————————— **10**

NOT-SO-GREAT   GREAT

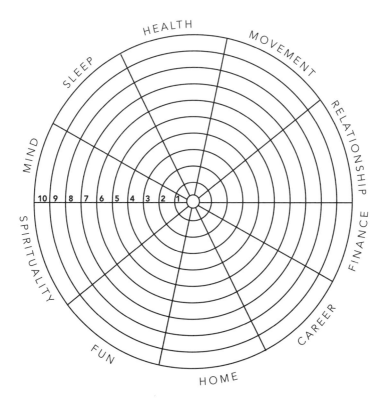

 Tip: *Use the space around the wheel to note ways in which you can add more balance to your life.*

MY AURA IS BRIGHT, BEAUTIFUL AND GLOWING

How am I feeling today?

Colour in how full your heart is and write out any emotions you are feeling today

_____

_____

_____

_____

No matter how big or small . . .

What do I love about the season I am in?

_____

_____

_____

What is something I am holding on to that I need to let go of?

_____

_____

_____

Have I taken care of my whole self today?

MIND 〇

BODY 〇

SPIRIT 〇

Write and release

Whatever is on your mind, write it out and let it go

_____

_____

_____

_____

I WELCOME THOUGHTS INTO MY LIFE THAT MATCH MY HIGH VIBRATIONS

How am I feeling today?

Colour in how full your heart is and write out any emotions you are feeling today

_____   ♡   _____
_____   _____

No matter how big or small . . .

My favourite part of the day is . . .

_____

_____

_____

If happiness were a colour, what would it be and why?

_____

_____

Have I taken care of my whole self today?

MIND ●

BODY ●

SPIRIT ●

Write and release

Whatever is on your mind, write it out and let it go

_____

_____

_____

_____

I FEEL LOVE AND COMPASSION FOR EVERYONE IN THE WORLD

How am I feeling today?

Colour in how full your heart is and write out any emotions you are feeling today

_____   ♡   _____

_____   _____

No matter how big or small . . .

I want to give more love to . . .

_____

_____

_____

What can I do to improve the relationship I have with myself?

_____

_____

_____

Have I taken care of my whole self today?

MIND ⬤

BODY ⬤

SPIRIT ⬤

Write and release

Whatever is on your mind, write it out and let it go

_____

_____

_____

_____

LOOKING OUT FOR LOVE

 Find the hearts. Not only in this journal, but look for hearts and heart-shaped things (clouds, leaves, anything you see!) in your day-to-day life. By doing this, you will slowly train your mind to look out for the love in your life.

I GIVE MYSELF THE CARE AND ATTENTION I DESERVE

How am I feeling today?

Colour in how full your heart is and write out any emotions you are feeling today

_____   _____

_____   _____

No matter how big or small . . .

What can I appreciate more about myself?

_____

_____

_____

In what areas in my life am I putting myself last and why?

_____

_____

_____

Have I taken care of my whole self today?

MIND

BODY

SPIRIT

Write and release

Whatever is on your mind, write it out and let it go

_____

_____

_____

_____

I TRUST IN THE BEAUTY OF DIVINE TIMING

How am I feeling today?

Colour in how full your heart is and write out any emotions you are feeling today

No matter how big or small . . .

What is something that makes me feel happy?

What is something that makes me feel sad?

Have I taken care of my whole self today?

MIND

BODY

SPIRIT

Write and release

Whatever is on your mind, write it out and let it go

EVERY DAY BRINGS WITH IT AN OPPORTUNITY TO BE HAPPY

How am I feeling today?

Colour in how full your heart is and write out any emotions you are feeling today

_____   ♡   _____
_____   _____

No matter how big or small . . .

What is one thing that I appreciate the most today?

_____

_____

_____

Are there any past events that I still blame myself for?

_____

_____

_____

Have I taken care of my whole self today?

MIND ⬤

BODY ⬤

SPIRIT ⬤

Write and release

Whatever is on your mind, write it out and let it go

_____

_____

_____

_____

GROUNDING

 Sometimes we can forget the beauty of being in the 'now'. Doing regular grounding exercises can help you feel calm and help your mind stay more focused on the present, rather than looking to the past or future.

5 THINGS I CAN SEE

4 THINGS I CAN FEEL

3 THINGS I CAN HEAR

2 THINGS I CAN SMELL

1 THING I CAN TASTE

Tip: Try this exercise whenever you are feeling overwhelmed.

I AM BEING GUIDED TO LIVE MY GREATEST LIFE

How am I feeling today?

Colour in how full your heart is and write out any emotions you are feeling today

_____ ♡ _____
_____   _____

No matter how big or small . . .

What is an achievement I am proud of?

_____

_____

_____

What would I do in my life if money were no object?

_____

_____

_____

Have I taken care of my whole self today?

MIND ●

BODY ●

SPIRIT ●

Write and release

Whatever is on your mind, write it out and let it go

_____

_____

_____

_____

ABUNDANCE IS COMING. I DESERVE IT. I ACCEPT IT.

How am I feeling today?

Colour in how full your heart is and write out any emotions you are feeling today

_____   ♡   _____
_____   _____

No matter how big or small . . .

What is a skill of mine that I would like to teach someone else?

_____

_____

_____

The last time I felt understood was . . .

_____

_____

_____

Have I taken care of my whole self today?

MIND ⚪

BODY ⚪

SPIRIT ⚪

Write and release

Whatever is on your mind, write it out and let it go

_____

_____

_____

_____

WHEN I TUNE INTO MY INNER SELF, I HEAR THE ANSWERS I NEED

How am I feeling today?

Colour in how full your heart is and write out any emotions you are feeling today

_____   ♡   _____
_____   _____

No matter how big or small . . .

What is something that makes me smile?

_____

_____

_____

What is one song that makes me feel good and why?

_____

_____

_____

Have I taken care of my whole self today?

MIND ●

BODY ●

SPIRIT ●

Write and release

Whatever is on your mind, write it out and let it go

_____

_____

_____

_____

GOOD VIBES PLAYLIST

 Create a playlist with songs that make you feel all those good vibes! Whenever you are feeling down, you can always come back to this.

My good vibes playlist

1
2
3
4
5
6
7
8
9
10

 Tip: *Feeling stuck? Check out our playlist on Spotify!*

I CHOOSE TO BE THE LIGHT IN ALL SITUATIONS

How am I feeling today?

Colour in how full your heart is and write out any emotions you are feeling today

_____   _____

_____   _____

No matter how big or small . . .

Who is someone that respects me?

_____

_____

_____

What is a mistake that helped me grow?

_____

_____

_____

Have I taken care of my whole self today?

MIND ⬤

BODY ⬤

SPIRIT ⬤

Write and release

Whatever is on your mind, write it out and let it go

_____

_____

_____

_____

I LOVE AND ACCEPT MYSELF FOR WHO I AM

How am I feeling today?

Colour in how full your heart is and write out any emotions you are feeling today

No matter how big or small . . .

A recent compliment that made me happy is . . .

_____

_____

_____

Is there an emotion that I try to avoid?

_____

_____

_____

Have I taken care of my whole self today?

MIND

BODY

SPIRIT

Write and release

Whatever is on your mind, write it out and let it go

_____

_____

_____

_____

EVERYTHING IS HAPPENING FOR ME, NOT TO ME

How am I feeling today?

Colour in how full your heart is and write out any emotions you are feeling today

_____   ♡   _____
_____   _____

No matter how big or small . . .

What is one beautiful thing I saw today?

_____

_____

_____

What is something that no longer makes me sad?

_____

_____

_____

Have I taken care of my whole self today?

MIND ●

BODY ●

SPIRIT ●

Write and release

Whatever is on your mind, write it out and let it go

_____

_____

_____

_____

GROUNDING BREATHWORK

Our breath is one thing that changes with every emotion. You may breathe faster when you are worried or skip a few breaths when you are excited. We may not be able to control our emotions at times, but we can take control of our breathing, which, in return, can help us feel a sense of calm.

Did you know that breathing out for longer (than breathing in) is proven to help relax the body?

Give this grounding breathwork exercise a go and always come back to it when you feel you may need it.

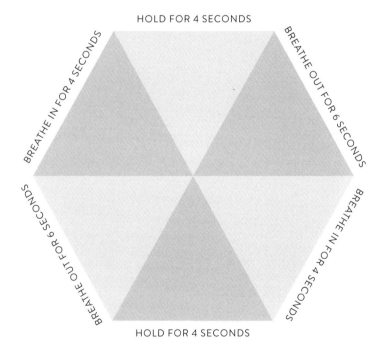

HOLD FOR 4 SECONDS

BREATHE IN FOR 4 SECONDS

BREATHE OUT FOR 6 SECONDS

BREATHE OUT FOR 6 SECONDS

BREATHE IN FOR 4 SECONDS

HOLD FOR 4 SECONDS

 Tip: *Add this exercise to your Calm Kit (page 22).*

I RADIATE SELF-LOVE AND CULTIVATE INNER HARMONY

How am I feeling today?

Colour in how full your heart is and write out any emotions you are feeling today

_____   _____

_____   _____

No matter how big or small . . .

What does love mean to me?

_____

_____

_____

Is there a relationship I need to nurture more?

_____

_____

_____

Have I taken care of my whole self today?

MIND ●

BODY ●

SPIRIT ●

Write and release

Whatever is on your mind, write it out and let it go

_____

_____

_____

_____

I AM POWERFUL ENOUGH TO CREATE THE LIFE I DESIRE

How am I feeling today?

Colour in how full your heart is and write out any emotions you are feeling today

_____   _____

_____   _____

No matter how big or small . . .

Who can I be my true authentic self around?

_____

_____

_____

What makes me feel free?

_____

_____

_____

Have I taken
care of my
whole self
today?

MIND

BODY

SPIRIT

Write and release

Whatever is on your mind, write it out and let it go

_____

_____

_____

_____

I CONTINUE TO MANIFEST SUCCESS IN MY LIFE

How am I feeling today?

Colour in how full your heart is and write out any emotions you are feeling today

_____ ♡ _____
_____   _____

No matter how big or small . . .

What is something that comforts me that I am grateful for?

_____

_____

_____

One positive change I can make today is . . .

_____

_____

_____

Have I taken care of my whole self today?

MIND ●

BODY ●

SPIRIT ●

Write and release
Whatever is on your mind, write it out and let it go

_____

_____

_____

_____

YOUR SPACE TO EXPRESS YOURSELF

Use this page to jot down thoughts, to-do lists, doodles – anything your heart or mind desires. This is your story to tell.

I CHOOSE TO LISTEN TO MY INTUITION RATHER THAN MY EGO

How am I feeling today?

Colour in how full your heart is and write out any emotions you are feeling today

_____   ♡   _____
_____   _____

No matter how big or small . . .

What is one opportunity I am grateful for?

_____

_____

_____

What lesson am I learning at this stage of my life?

_____

_____

_____

Have I taken care of my whole self today?

MIND ●

BODY ●

SPIRIT ●

Write and release

Whatever is on your mind, write it out and let it go

_____

_____

_____

_____

TODAY IS _____

I AM CAPABLE OF ACHIEVING ANYTHING I SET MY MIND TO

How am I feeling today?

Colour in how full your heart is and write out any emotions you are feeling today

_____

_____

_____

_____

No matter how big or small . . .

What is the kindest thing I have done for myself?

_____

_____

_____

Who is someone I need an apology from and why?

_____

_____

_____

Have I taken care of my whole self today?

MIND ○

BODY ○

SPIRIT ○

Write and release

Whatever is on your mind, write it out and let it go

_____

_____

_____

_____

I AM FREE TO BE MYSELF

How am I feeling today?

Colour in how full your heart is and write out any emotions you are feeling today

_____   ♡   _____
_____   _____

No matter how big or small . . .

A freedom I am grateful for is . . .

_____

_____

_____

Is there something or someone I think about every day?

_____

_____

_____

Have I taken
care of my
whole self
today?

Write and release

Whatever is on your mind, write it out and let it go

MIND ⬤

BODY ⬤

SPIRIT ⬤

_____

_____

_____

_____

KINDNESS CHALLENGE

 Challenge yourself to spread some kindness today. Tick any of the below that you have managed to do recently. (One is left blank for you to fill in with something that is personal to you.)

GIVE SOMEONE
A COMPLIMENT

HOLD THE DOOR
OPEN FOR
SOMEONE

OFFER TO PAY
FOR SOMEONE'S
MEAL/DRINK

PERFORM A RANDOM
ACT OF KINDNESS

SHARE YOUR SMILE WITH SOMEONE

TAKE SOME ITEMS
TO A CHARITY SHOP

I GENERATE POSITIVITY WITH EVERY BREATH I TAKE

How am I feeling today?

Colour in how full your heart is and write out any emotions you are feeling today

_____ ♡ _____

_____   _____

No matter how big or small . . .

Who is someone that makes me feel alive?

_____

_____

_____

What do I like doing when I need to recharge?

_____

_____

_____

Have I taken care of my whole self today?

MIND ⬤

BODY ⬤

SPIRIT ⬤

Write and release

Whatever is on your mind, write it out and let it go

_____

_____

_____

_____

I AM MAKING SPACE FOR NEW ENERGY TO ENTER AND FILL MY LIFE WITH JOY

How am I feeling today?

Colour in how full your heart is and write out any emotions you are feeling today

_____   _____

_____   _____

No matter how big or small . . .

Who gives the best hugs?

_____

_____

_____

What advice can I give someone going through the same thing as me?

_____

_____

_____

Have I taken
care of my
whole self
today?

Write and release

Whatever is on your mind, write it out and let it go

MIND

BODY

SPIRIT

I DESERVE EVERYTHING THAT I DESIRE

How am I feeling today?

Colour in how full your heart is and write out any emotions you are feeling today

_____

_____

_____

_____

No matter how big or small . . .

What is a small moment that means a lot to me?

_____

_____

_____

Is there anything I find difficult to open up about?

_____

_____

_____

Have I taken care of my whole self today?

MIND

BODY

SPIRIT

Write and release

Whatever is on your mind, write it out and let it go

_____

_____

_____

_____

RESET YOUR MIND

 If you are ever feeling overwhelmed, try some mind-reset techniques to help you release some of the tension and feel at ease.

Try box breathing (p. 43)

Do some gentle stretching or yoga asana

Organize your space (e.g. room, desk)

Revisit your bucket list (p. 99) and reverse bucket list (p. 26)

Leave a whole day unplanned for yourself

Do a social media cleanse (e.g. unfollow accounts that no longer resonate with you)

Reply to emails and messages

Spend some time in nature by going for a walk

Listen to our ten-minute guided meditation on our YouTube Channel

I AM A UNIQUE AND CREATIVE SOUL

How am I feeling today?

Colour in how full your heart is and write out any emotions you are feeling today

_____   ♡   _____
_____   _____

No matter how big or small . . .

What does happiness mean to me?

_____

_____

_____

What makes me unique?

_____

_____

_____

Have I taken care of my whole self today?

MIND ●

BODY ●

SPIRIT ●

Write and release

Whatever is on your mind, write it out and let it go

_____

_____

_____

_____

I AIM TO LIVE WITH PURPOSE WITH EVERY ACTION I TAKE

How am I feeling today?

Colour in how full your heart is and write out any emotions you are feeling today

_____   ♡   _____

_____   _____

No matter how big or small . . .

Someone I admire is . . .

_____

_____

_____

If I was given the chance to fix one mistake, what would it be and why?

_____

_____

_____

Have I taken care of my whole self today?

MIND ●

BODY ●

SPIRIT ●

Write and release

Whatever is on your mind, write it out and let it go

_____

_____

_____

_____

LIFE IS AN ADVENTURE AND I AM READY FOR THE RIDE

How am I feeling today?

Colour in how full your heart is and write out any emotions you are feeling today

_____   _____

_____   _____

No matter how big or small . . .

Who is someone that makes me feel motivated and why?

_____

_____

_____

What do I feel strongly about?

_____

_____

_____

Have I taken care of my whole self today?

MIND ⬤

BODY ⬤

SPIRIT ⬤

Write and release

Whatever is on your mind, write it out and let it go

_____

_____

_____

_____

AFFIRM IT

Affirming positive thoughts can have transformative effects. Write out and repeat the affirmation below.

I AM DRIVEN

I AM PROUD OF MYSELF AND HOW FAR I HAVE COME

How am I feeling today?

Colour in how full your heart is and write out any emotions you are feeling today

_____   ♡   _____

_____   _____

No matter how big or small . . .

What is something that has helped me during a difficult time?

_____

_____

_____

Where do I need more balance in my life?

_____

_____

_____

Have I taken care of my whole self today?

MIND ⬤

BODY ⬤

SPIRIT ⬤

Write and release

Whatever is on your mind, write it out and let it go

_____

_____

_____

_____

MY HEART AND MIND ARE FREE FROM ALL NEGATIVITY

How am I feeling today?

Colour in how full your heart is and write out any emotions you are feeling today

_____   _____

_____   _____

No matter how big or small . . .

What is a colour that makes me feel good?

_____

_____

_____

I enter a room with everyone I know. Who do I seek first and why?

_____

_____

_____

Have I taken care of my whole self today?

MIND

BODY

SPIRIT

Write and release

Whatever is on your mind, write it out and let it go

_____

_____

_____

_____

I AM HERE, I AM PRESENT AND I AM SAFE

How am I feeling today?

Colour in how full your heart is and write out any emotions you are feeling today

_____   ♡   _____
_____   _____

No matter how big or small . . .

What is something I loved about yesterday?

_____
_____
_____

If I could only keep three things right now, what would they be and why?

_____
_____
_____

Have I taken care of my whole self today?

MIND 🔘

BODY 🔘

SPIRIT 🔘

Write and release

Whatever is on your mind, write it out and let it go

_____
_____
_____
_____

MINDFUL COLOURING

 Colouring is a great way to get into a meditative state by calming the mind and feeling relaxed. Let your creativity flow and colour the below.

EACH DAY IS A GIFT AND I ACCEPT IT WITH GRATITUDE

How am I feeling today?

Colour in how full your heart is and write out any emotions you are feeling today

_____   ♡   _____

No matter how big or small . . .

A small joy I would like to savour is . . .

_____

_____

_____

How has the weather made me feel today?

_____

_____

_____

Have I taken care of my whole self today?

MIND ⬤

BODY ⬤

SPIRIT ⬤

Write and release

Whatever is on your mind, write it out and let it go

_____

_____

_____

_____

I LOVE MYSELF IMMENSELY

How am I feeling today?

Colour in how full your heart is and write out any emotions you are feeling today

_____   _____
_____   _____

No matter how big or small . . .

How can I show kindness to someone I love?

_____

_____

_____

What is something I wish someone would do for me?

_____

_____

_____

Have I taken care of my whole self today?

MIND

BODY

SPIRIT

Write and release

Whatever is on your mind, write it out and let it go

_____

_____

_____

_____

I AM GRATEFUL FOR THE GIFT OF BEING ALIVE

How am I feeling today?

Colour in how full your heart is and write out any emotions you are feeling today

_____   _____

_____   _____

No matter how big or small . . .

What are three things I am grateful for?

_____

_____

_____

What do I love doing when I just want to have fun?

_____

_____

_____

Have I taken care of my whole self today?

MIND ●

BODY ●

SPIRIT ●

Write and release

Whatever is on your mind, write it out and let it go

_____

_____

_____

_____

MY LIFE WHEEL

On a scale from 1 to 10, how am I feeling in the following areas of my life?
Do not overthink it, just colour it in!

1 ———————————————————————— **10**
NOT-SO-GREAT   GREAT

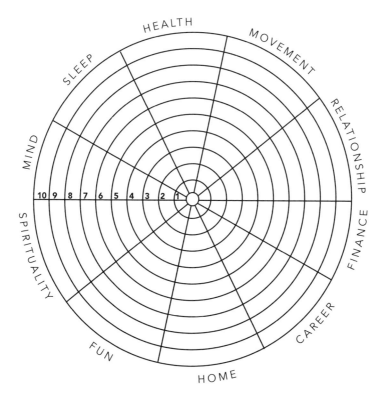

Tip: *Use the space around the wheel to note ways in which you can add more balance to your life.*

I AM MY OWN BEST FRIEND

How am I feeling today?

Colour in how full your heart is and write out any emotions you are feeling today

_____ ♡ _____
_____   _____

No matter how big or small . . .

Describe a time I really felt loved.

_____

_____

_____

Is there anything I am insecure about?

_____

_____

_____

Have I taken
care of my
whole self
today?

MIND ⬤

BODY ⬤

SPIRIT ⬤

Write and release

Whatever is on your mind, write it out and let it go

_____

_____

_____

_____

I AM OVERFLOWING WITH JOY AND ABUNDANCE

How am I feeling today?

Colour in how full your heart is and write out any emotions you are feeling today

No matter how big or small . . .

What is one quote or saying that inspires me?

What kind of a friend am I and what can I do to be a better one?

Have I taken
care of my
whole self
today?

MIND

BODY

SPIRIT

Write and release

Whatever is on your mind, write it out and let it go

MY HEART IS OPEN TO RECEIVING LOVE

How am I feeling today?

Colour in how full your heart is and write out any emotions you are feeling today

_____   _____

_____   _____

No matter how big or small . . .

Who is someone I have not said thank you to in a while?

_____

_____

_____

What is one thing I want to manifest in my life?

_____

_____

_____

Have I taken care of my whole self today?

MIND

BODY

SPIRIT

Write and release

Whatever is on your mind, write it out and let it go

_____

_____

_____

_____

WORD SCRAMBLE

 Unscramble to unveil the powerful words below.

OGDO IEVSB ➡️

GNINTSIFAME IGAMC ➡️

CATTTRA ACENUBNDA ➡️

EIVNID IGTINM ➡️

IERATAD VIOTITPISY ➡️

MY BODY IS SACRED; I WILL TAKE CARE OF IT

How am I feeling today?

Colour in how full your heart is and write out any emotions you are feeling today

_____   ♡   _____
_____   _____

No matter how big or small . . .

What is one item I treasure the most?

_____

_____

_____

What is something I wish I had known sooner?

_____

_____

_____

Have I taken care of my whole self today?

MIND ●

BODY ●

SPIRIT ●

Write and release

Whatever is on your mind, write it out and let it go

_____

_____

_____

_____

MY LOVE FOR MYSELF IS MY BIGGEST STRENGTH

How am I feeling today?

Colour in how full your heart is and write out any emotions you are feeling today

No matter how big or small . . .

A beautiful blessing in disguise I have experienced is . . .

Is there anything that is draining my energy?

Have I taken care of my whole self today?

MIND

BODY

SPIRIT

Write and release

Whatever is on your mind, write it out and let it go

I RELEASE ALL THAT IS NOT SERVING ME

How am I feeling today?

Colour in how full your heart is and write out any emotions you are feeling today

_____   ♡   _____

_____   _____

No matter how big or small . . .

What keeps me grounded?

_____

_____

_____

Today and always, I am . . .

_____

_____

_____

Have I taken care of my whole self today?

MIND ●

BODY ●

SPIRIT ●

Write and release

Whatever is on your mind, write it out and let it go

_____

_____

_____

_____

MY PEOPLE

Who are three people in your life that you absolutely adore and why?
If you have not told them that you love them recently, this is your
chance to do so.

NAME	WHY DO I LOVE THEM?	HAVE I TOLD THEM?

NAME	WHY DO I LOVE THEM?	HAVE I TOLD THEM?

NAME	WHY DO I LOVE THEM?	HAVE I TOLD THEM?

I BELIEVE IN MYSELF AND KNOW THAT ANYTHING IS POSSIBLE

How am I feeling today?

Colour in how full your heart is and write out any emotions you are feeling today

_____   _____

_____   _____

No matter how big or small . . .

On a scale from 1 to 10, how grateful do I feel today and why?

_____

_____

_____

I wish I had more love for . . .

_____

_____

_____

Have I taken care of my whole self today?

MIND ⬤

BODY ⬤

SPIRIT ⬤

Write and release

Whatever is on your mind, write it out and let it go

_____

_____

_____

_____

I AM EXCITED ABOUT MY FUTURE AND MOTIVATED BY MY DREAMS

How am I feeling today?

Colour in how full your heart is and write out any emotions you are feeling today

_____   ♡   _____
_____   _____

No matter how big or small . . .

What are three things about myself that I am proud of?

_____

_____

_____

What is something I want to experience at least once in my life?

_____

_____

_____

Have I taken care of my whole self today?

MIND ⬤

BODY ⬤

SPIRIT ⬤

Write and release

Whatever is on your mind, write it out and let it go

_____

_____

_____

_____

MY WORDS, EMOTIONS, THOUGHTS AND ACTIONS ARE ALIGNED TO GREATNESS

How am I feeling today?

Colour in how full your heart is and write out any emotions you are feeling today

_____   _____

_____   _____

No matter how big or small . . .

Someone that I trust is . . .

_____

_____

_____

What is my favourite colour and how does it make me feel?

_____

_____

_____

Have I taken
care of my
whole self
today?

Write and release

Whatever is on your mind, write it out and let it go

MIND

BODY

SPIRIT

_____

_____

_____

_____

COLOURING QUOTE

 Colouring is a great way to get into a meditative state by calming the mind and feeling relaxed. Visualize and feel the words below as you colour.

I AM CONSTANTLY GROWING AND EVOLVING

How am I feeling today?

Colour in how full your heart is and write out any emotions you are feeling today

_____   _____

_____   _____

No matter how big or small . . .

Today was great because . . .

_____

_____

_____

What are three things that make my life easier?

_____

_____

_____

Have I taken care of my whole self today?

MIND

BODY

SPIRIT

Write and release

Whatever is on your mind, write it out and let it go

_____

_____

_____

_____

I MAKE DEEP, MEANINGFUL CONNECTIONS

How am I feeling today?

Colour in how full your heart is and write out any emotions you are feeling today

_____   ♡   _____
_____   _____

No matter how big or small . . .

Who is that one person that makes my day happier?

_____

_____

_____

I am going to be gentle with myself because . . .

_____

_____

_____

Have I taken
care of my
whole self
today?

Write and release

Whatever is on your mind, write it out and let it go

MIND ○   _____

BODY ○   _____

SPIRIT ○   _____

                      _____

I TREAT MY BODY WITH LOVE AND RESPECT

How am I feeling today?

Colour in how full your heart is and write out any emotions you are feeling today

_____   ♡   _____
_____   _____

No matter how big or small . . .

I love my body because . . .

_____

_____

_____

I feel amazing when I . . .

_____

_____

_____

Have I taken care of my whole self today?

MIND ●

BODY ●

SPIRIT ●

Write and release

Whatever is on your mind, write it out and let it go

_____

_____

_____

_____

BODY POSITIVITY

We tend to compare our physical bodies to the people we see around us, in the media and even online. We forget to appreciate the body we have and all the incredible things our body does for us every day. Each and every one of us is so uniquely beautiful, so let us practise some self-love by adding responses to the below.

WHAT I LOVE
ABOUT MY BODY:

THINGS THAT MAKE
ME UNIQUE:

I CAN HELP MY
BODY BY DOING:

MY BODY HELPS
ME TO:

I HAVE THE POTENTIAL AND SKILLS TO ACHIEVE MY DESIRES

How am I feeling today?

Colour in how full your heart is and write out any emotions you are feeling today

_____

_____

No matter how big or small . . .

A memory that makes me happy is . . .

_____

_____

_____

How does life feel right now?

_____

_____

_____

Have I taken care of my whole self today?

MIND

BODY

SPIRIT

Write and release

Whatever is on your mind, write it out and let it go

_____

_____

_____

_____

I AM CREATING A POSITIVE FUTURE FOR MYSELF

How am I feeling today?

Colour in how full your heart is and write out any emotions you are feeling today

_____   _____

_____   _____

No matter how big or small . . .

Simple moments I treasure are...

_____

_____

_____

Is there anything I am scared to say?

_____

_____

_____

Have I taken care of my whole self today?	Write and release
	Whatever is on your mind, write it out and let it go

Have I taken
care of my
whole self
today?

MIND ⬤

BODY ⬤

SPIRIT ⬤

Write and release
Whatever is on your mind, write it out and let it go

_____

_____

_____

_____

_____

I AM WILLING TO SEE WHERE AND HOW I NEED TO CHANGE

How am I feeling today?

Colour in how full your heart is and write out any emotions you are feeling today

_____   _____
_____   _____

No matter how big or small . . .

What is one thing I love about my personality?

_____

_____

_____

If I could change one habit, what would it be and why?

_____

_____

_____

Have I taken care of my whole self today?

MIND

BODY

SPIRIT

Write and release

Whatever is on your mind, write it out and let it go

_____

_____

_____

_____

HABIT SWAP

 Are there any habits you are trying to change? Write down three habits you would like to change and, for each, think of a more positive, fulfilling action you could do instead.

1 _____ ➡ _____
                              _____
                              _____
                              _____
                              _____

2 _____ ➡ _____
                              _____
                              _____
                              _____
                              _____

3 _____ ➡ _____
                              _____
                              _____

WHAT IS MEANT TO BE MINE IS ALREADY MAKING ITS WAY TO ME

How am I feeling today?

Colour in how full your heart is and write out any emotions you are feeling today

_____

_____

_____

_____

No matter how big or small . . .

What is one thing that I can proudly talk about?

_____

_____

_____

What is something I cannot stop thinking about?

_____

_____

_____

Have I taken care of my whole self today?

MIND

BODY

SPIRIT

Write and release

Whatever is on your mind, write it out and let it go

_____

_____

_____

_____

I DESERVE ALL THE GOOD THINGS LIFE HAS TO OFFER

How am I feeling today?

Colour in how full your heart is and write out any emotions you are feeling today

_____   ♡   _____
_____   _____

No matter how big or small . . .

What is one of my favourite things I own and why?

_____
_____
_____

Am I living in the moment or for the moment?

_____
_____
_____

Have I taken care of my whole self today?

MIND ⬤

BODY ⬤

SPIRIT ⬤

Write and release

Whatever is on your mind, write it out and let it go

_____
_____
_____
_____

I EXPRESS GRATITUDE DAILY

How am I feeling today?

Colour in how full your heart is and write out any emotions you are feeling today

_____

_____

No matter how big or small . . .

What is my favourite way to connect with loved ones?

_____

_____

_____

When was the last time I planned an activity with a friend?

_____

_____

_____

Have I taken care of my whole self today?

MIND

BODY

SPIRIT

Write and release

Whatever is on your mind, write it out and let it go

_____

_____

_____

_____

60-MINUTE SELF-CARE CHALLENGE

 Challenge yourself to have a great day. Try and do the following sixty-minute self-care challenge.

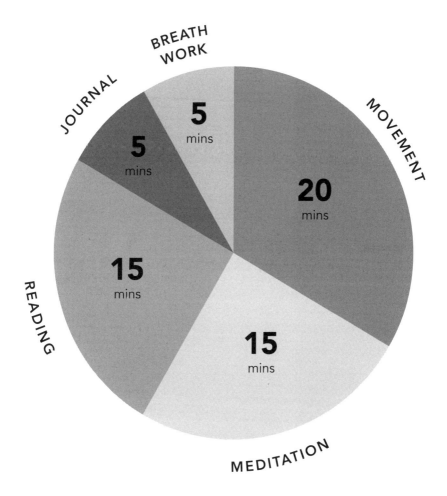

I WELCOME CHANGE WITH OPEN ARMS

How am I feeling today?

Colour in how full your heart is and write out any emotions you are feeling today

_____

_____

_____

_____

No matter how big or small . . .

What is a moment in my life that I would want to relive again?

_____

_____

_____

To me, unconditional love means . . .

_____

_____

_____

Have I taken care of my whole self today?

MIND ⬤

BODY ⬤

SPIRIT ⬤

Write and release

Whatever is on your mind, write it out and let it go

_____

_____

_____

_____

MY ABILITY TO CONQUER MY CHALLENGES IS LIMITLESS

How am I feeling today?

Colour in how full your heart is and write out any emotions you are feeling today

No matter how big or small . . .

My favourite part of journaling so far is . . .

I know I am growing when . . .

Have I taken care of my whole self today?

MIND

BODY

SPIRIT

Write and release

Whatever is on your mind, write it out and let it go

I AM SHAPING MY REALITY WITH MY POSITIVITY EVERY DAY

How am I feeling today?

Colour in how full your heart is and write out any emotions you are feeling today

No matter how big or small . . .

An activity that makes me feel good is . . .

What is one thing I can truly do for myself this week?

Have I taken care of my whole self today?

MIND

BODY

SPIRIT

Write and release

Whatever is on your mind, write it out and let it go

FEEL-GOOD FOLDER

Something we always have with us is our phone. Although social media can be a great source of inspiration, creating your very own Feel-Good Folder as a photo album can give you a personalized feed of content, photos, videos and even memories that lift your spirits!

Step 1:

Create a Feel-Good Folder in your photo albums.

Step 2:

Add screenshots of posts or your own photos and videos that bring you joy and warmth to the folder. Continue to update this folder by adding new content to it.

Step 3:

If you are having a hard day or tough time, scroll through this personalized album of content to uplift your energy and mood.

 Tip: Add your Feel-Good Folder to your Calm Kit (page 22).

EACH DAY IS AN OPPORTUNITY TO START AFRESH

How am I feeling today?

Colour in how full your heart is and write out any emotions you are feeling today

_____

_____   _____

_____

No matter how big or small . . .

What is a holiday that I am grateful for?

_____

_____

_____

What feels like home to me?

_____

_____

_____

Have I taken
care of my
whole self
today?

MIND ◉

BODY ◉

SPIRIT ◉

Write and release

Whatever is on your mind, write it out and let it go

_____

_____

_____

_____

I BELIEVE IN MYSELF AND MY ABILITY TO SUCCEED

How am I feeling today?

Colour in how full your heart is and write out any emotions you are feeling today

_____

_____

_____

_____

No matter how big or small . . .

What is a positive memory I want to create?

What do I value most in a friendship?

Have I taken care of my whole self today?

MIND

BODY

SPIRIT

Write and release

Whatever is on your mind, write it out and let it go

MY POWER AND POTENTIAL ARE UNLIMITED

How am I feeling today?

Colour in how full your heart is and write out any emotions you are feeling today

_____   _____

_____   _____

No matter how big or small . . .

What is my greatest talent?

_____

_____

_____

Do I set high standards for others and/or myself? Why?

_____

_____

_____

Have I taken care of my whole self today?

MIND ⬤

BODY ⬤

SPIRIT ⬤

Write and release

Whatever is on your mind, write it out and let it go

_____

_____

_____

_____

MY LOVE LIST

 Write down anything and everything that you love. It can be people, places, things, colours or experiences. Anything that makes your heart happy.

e.g. Having a bubble bath

1.

2.

3.

4.

5.

6.

7.

8.

9.

10.

I AM READY TO RECEIVE GOOD HEALTH, WEALTH AND LOVE

How am I feeling today?

Colour in how full your heart is and write out any emotions you are feeling today

_____ ♡ _____

No matter how big or small . . .

I feel open when . . .

_____

_____

_____

What is something that I am holding on to that is holding me back?

_____

_____

_____

Have I taken care of my whole self today?

MIND ●

BODY ●

SPIRIT ●

Write and release

Whatever is on your mind, write it out and let it go

_____

_____

_____

_____

I TRUST MY ABILITY TO LET GO OF SUFFERING AND EMOTIONAL PAIN

How am I feeling today?

Colour in how full your heart is and write out any emotions you are feeling today

_____   _____

_____   _____

No matter how big or small . . .

What makes me feel valued?

_____

_____

_____

Do I listen to my head or my heart?

_____

_____

_____

Have I taken care of my whole self today?

MIND

BODY

SPIRIT

Write and release

Whatever is on your mind, write it out and let it go

_____

_____

_____

_____

MY STRENGTH IS GREATER THAN ANY STRUGGLE

How am I feeling today?

Colour in how full your heart is and write out any emotions you are feeling today

_____   _____
_____   _____

No matter how big or small . . .

What is something that cheers me up on a rough day?

_____

_____

_____

What is the best piece of advice I can give to myself?

_____

_____

_____

Have I taken care of my whole self today?

MIND ●

BODY ●

SPIRIT ●

Write and release

Whatever is on your mind, write it out and let it go

_____

_____

_____

_____

I . . .

Finish the sentence with as little or as much as you wish.

I EXPERIENCE

I GENERATE

I HAVE

I HOPE

I BELIEVE IN

I WANT

I EXPRESS IMMENSE GRATITUDE TO OTHERS FOR THEIR KINDNESS

How am I feeling today?

Colour in how full your heart is and write out any emotions you are feeling today

_____   _____

_____   _____

No matter how big or small . . .

Who is someone in my life I take for granted?

_____

_____

_____

How is the public me different from the private me?

_____

_____

_____

Have I taken care of my whole self today?

MIND

BODY

SPIRIT

Write and release

Whatever is on your mind, write it out and let it go

_____

_____

_____

_____

I ACCEPT EVERY CORNER OF MY BEING WITH LOVE

How am I feeling today?

Colour in how full your heart is and write out any emotions you are feeling today

_____   _____

_____   _____

No matter how big or small . . .

How can I positively impact someone else's day?

_____

_____

_____

Is it important what people think of me?

_____

_____

_____

Have I taken care of my whole self today?

MIND

BODY

SPIRIT

Write and release

Whatever is on your mind, write it out and let it go

_____

_____

_____

_____

GROWTH IS A CONSTANT IN MY LIFE AND I AM HERE FOR IT

How am I feeling today?

Colour in how full your heart is and write out any emotions you are feeling today

_____   _____
_____   _____

No matter how big or small . . .

My favourite day of the week is . . .

_____

_____

_____

What am I committed to making happen no matter what?

_____

_____

_____

Have I taken care of my whole self today?

MIND

BODY

SPIRIT

Write and release

Whatever is on your mind, write it out and let it go

_____

_____

_____

_____

MY LIFE WHEEL

On a scale from 1 to 10, how am I feeling in the following areas of my life? Do not overthink it, just colour it in!

1 ———————————————————— **10**

NOT-SO-GREAT   GREAT

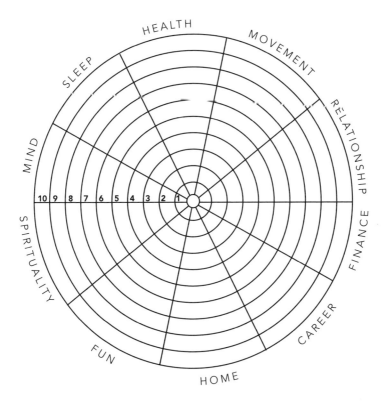

Tip: *Use the space around the wheel to note ways in which you can add more balance to your life.*

I WAKE UP EVERY MORNING CHOOSING PEACE

How am I feeling today?

Colour in how full your heart is and write out any emotions you are feeling today

_____   ♡   _____
_____   _____

No matter how big or small . . .

What is something that makes me feel safe?

_____

_____

_____

What is something I would tell my younger self to appreciate more?

_____

_____

_____

Have I taken care of my whole self today?

MIND ●

BODY ●

SPIRIT ●

Write and release

Whatever is on your mind, write it out and let it go

_____

_____

_____

_____

I AM STRONG AND CAN OVERCOME ANY CHALLENGE

How am I feeling today?

Colour in how full your heart is and write out any emotions you are feeling today

No matter how big or small . . .

Someone I like to keep close to my heart is . . .

How would I describe myself in one sentence?

Have I taken care of my whole self today?

MIND

BODY

SPIRIT

Write and release

Whatever is on your mind, write it out and let it go

MY GOALS GRAVITATE NATURALLY TOWARDS ME

How am I feeling today?

Colour in how full your heart is and write out any emotions you are feeling today

_____   ♡   _____
_____   _____

No matter how big or small . . .

Happiness feels like . . .

_____

_____

_____

When I look in the mirror I see . . .

_____

_____

_____

Have I taken care of my whole self today?

MIND ●

BODY ●

SPIRIT ●

Write and release

Whatever is on your mind, write it out and let it go

_____

_____

_____

_____

MIRROR WORK

The mirror work technique, popularized by Louise Hay, has many incredible benefits, and creates a powerful connection to an affirmation as you can physically see yourself in the mirror while you say it.

Below are some simple mirror work affirmations to try out. They work best when you say them daily, so give it a try and see how this exercise can shift your energy for the better!

I am worthy of love

My opinion matters

I am in charge of how I feel today

I am unique, talented and beautiful

I choose joy

I am grateful for my body

I love the person I am becoming

I validate myself and that is enough

I breathe in calm every day

I accept my mistakes and grow every day

I am doing the best I can

I am filled with hope

I am surrounded by healing energies

I am strong, happy and enough

I CELEBRATE MY INNER AND OUTER BODY

How am I feeling today?

Colour in how full your heart is and write out any emotions you are feeling today

_____   _____

_____   ♡   _____

No matter how big or small . . .

I am excited about . . .

_____

_____

_____

What do I see myself doing in ten years' time?

_____

_____

_____

Have I taken care of my whole self today?

MIND ●

BODY ●

SPIRIT ●

Write and release

Whatever is on your mind, write it out and let it go

_____

_____

_____

_____

THE UNIVERSE SUPPORTS ME IN EVERYTHING I DO

How am I feeling today?

Colour in how full your heart is and write out any emotions you are feeling today

No matter how big or small . . .

I feel appreciated when . . .

Who is someone I looked up to as a child and why?

Have I taken
care of my
whole self
today?

MIND

BODY

SPIRIT

Write and release

Whatever is on your mind, write it out and let it go

EVERY CELL IN MY BODY IS VIBRATING WITH GRATITUDE AND LOVE

How am I feeling today?

Colour in how full your heart is and write out any emotions you are feeling today

_____   ♡   _____

_____   _____

No matter how big or small . . .

I am grateful for this journey because . . .

_____

_____

_____

Is there anything I waste my time on? Why might this be?

_____

_____

_____

Have I taken care of my whole self today?

MIND ●

BODY ●

SPIRIT ●

Write and release

Whatever is on your mind, write it out and let it go

_____

_____

_____

_____

GROUNDING

Sometimes we can forget the beauty of being in the 'now'. Doing regular grounding exercises can help you feel calm and help your mind stay more focused on the present, rather than looking to the past or future.

5 THINGS I CAN SEE

4 THINGS I CAN FEEL

3 THINGS I CAN HEAR

2 THINGS I CAN SMELL

1 THING I CAN TASTE

 Tip: *Try this exercise whenever you are feeling overwhelmed.*

EVERYTHING I AM SEARCHING FOR IS ALREADY WITHIN ME

How am I feeling today?

Colour in how full your heart is and write out any emotions you are feeling today

_____   ♡   _____
_____   _____

No matter how big or small . . .

What is my place of happiness?

_____
_____
_____

Who is someone I have known for a long time? How do they make me feel?

_____
_____
_____

Have I taken care of my whole self today?

MIND ●

BODY ●

SPIRIT ●

Write and release

Whatever is on your mind, write it out and let it go

_____
_____
_____
_____

I ILLUMINATE THE LIVES OF EVERYONE I MEET

How am I feeling today?

Colour in how full your heart is and write out any emotions you are feeling today

_____   ♡   _____

_____   _____

No matter how big or small . . .

What is something someone told me that changed my perspective on life?

_____

_____

_____

How can I encourage myself to get outside of my comfort zone?

_____

_____

_____

Have I taken care of my whole self today?

MIND ⚪

BODY ⚪

SPIRIT ⚪

Write and release

Whatever is on your mind, write it out and let it go

_____

_____

_____

_____

I FULLY SURRENDER MY DESIRES AND TRUST THE UNFOLDING OF MY LIFE

How am I feeling today?

Colour in how full your heart is and write out any emotions you are feeling today

_____   _____

_____   _____

No matter how big or small . . .

I feel relaxed when . . .

_____

_____

_____

Do I find it difficult to let things go? How can I make this easier for myself?

_____

_____

_____

Have I taken care of my whole self today?

MIND

BODY

SPIRIT

Write and release

Whatever is on your mind, write it out and let it go

_____

_____

_____

_____

DOT-TO-DOT

Join the dots to reveal the message.

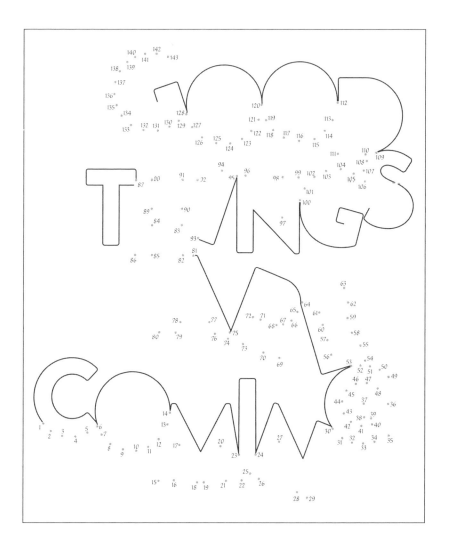

I ALWAYS TREAT MYSELF WITH LOVE AND COMPASSION

How am I feeling today?

Colour in how full your heart is and write out any emotions you are feeling today

_____   ♡   _____

_____   _____

No matter how big or small . . .

The best job I have ever had was . . .

_____

_____

_____

What is something I can do when I next feel overwhelmed?

_____

_____

_____

Have I taken care of my whole self today?

MIND ●

BODY ●

SPIRIT ●

Write and release

Whatever is on your mind, write it out and let it go

_____

_____

_____

_____

I AM CAPABLE OF LETTING GO OF UNHEALTHY ATTACHMENTS

How am I feeling today?

Colour in how full your heart is and write out any emotions you are feeling today

_____   ♡   _____
_____   _____

No matter how big or small . . .

A time I felt courageous was . . .

_____
_____
_____

Where is my heart pulling me?

_____
_____
_____

Have I taken care of my whole self today?

MIND ●

BODY ●

SPIRIT ●

Write and release

Whatever is on your mind, write it out and let it go

_____
_____
_____
_____

I HONOUR AND UPHOLD MY BOUNDARIES WHILE RESPECTING OTHER PEOPLE

How am I feeling today?

Colour in how full your heart is and write out any emotions you are feeling today

_____   _____

_____   _____

No matter how big or small . . .

What is something people appreciate about me?

_____

_____

_____

What is a boundary that I need to reinforce?

_____

_____

_____

Have I taken
care of my
whole self
today?

MIND

BODY

SPIRIT

Write and release

Whatever is on your mind, write it out and let it go

_____

_____

_____

_____

3 THINGS

 Message your loved ones (as many as you like) and ask them to positively describe you in three words. Write these words inside the heart below.

 Tip: *Add this exercise to your Calm Kit (page 22) and come back to it when you are next feeling low.*

I OWN MY POWER AND USE MY VOICE TO UPLIFT MYSELF AND OTHERS

How am I feeling today?

Colour in how full your heart is and write out any emotions you are feeling today

_____   _____

No matter how big or small . . .

A positive way I have changed is . . .

_____

_____

_____

Who is my authentic self?

_____

_____

_____

Have I taken care of my whole self today?

MIND ⬤

BODY ⬤

SPIRIT ⬤

Write and release

Whatever is on your mind, write it out and let it go

_____

_____

_____

_____

MY BODY IS POWERFUL AND KNOWS HOW TO HEAL ITSELF

How am I feeling today?

Colour in how full your heart is and write out any emotions you are feeling today

_____   _____

_____   _____

No matter how big or small . . .

My heart feels full when . . .

_____

_____

_____

Do I stand up for myself and how does that make me feel?

_____

_____

_____

Have I taken care of my whole self today?

MIND

BODY

SPIRIT

Write and release

Whatever is on your mind, write it out and let it go

_____

_____

_____

_____

I AM NOT MY THOUGHTS AND THEY DO NOT DEFINE ME

How am I feeling today?

Colour in how full your heart is and write out any emotions you are feeling today

_____   _____

_____   _____

No matter how big or small . . .

Who is someone that allows me to be myself?

_____

_____

_____

Would I rather spend a day with my younger or older self and why?

_____

_____

_____

Have I taken care of my whole self today?

MIND ⬤

BODY ⬤

SPIRIT ⬤

Write and release

Whatever is on your mind, write it out and let it go

_____

_____

_____

_____

YOUR SPACE TO EXPRESS YOURSELF

Use this page to jot down thoughts, to-do lists, doodles – anything your heart or mind desires. This is your story to tell.

I FEEL SECURE IN WHO I AM AND DO NOT NEED TO COMPARE MYSELF TO OTHERS

How am I feeling today?

Colour in how full your heart is and write out any emotions you are feeling today

_____

_____

_____

_____

No matter how big or small . . .

What is something I use every day that I am grateful for?

_____

_____

If I were a type of weather, what would I be and why?

_____

_____

_____

Have I taken care of my whole self today?

MIND ●

BODY ●

SPIRIT ●

Write and release

Whatever is on your mind, write it out and let it go

_____

_____

_____

_____

MY RELATIONSHIPS ARE STABLE AND HEALTHY

How am I feeling today?

Colour in how full your heart is and write out any emotions you are feeling today

_____   ♡   _____

No matter how big or small . . .

A fear I have overcome is . . .

_____

_____

_____

How do I handle a situation when someone has a different opinion to me?

_____

_____

_____

Have I taken
care of my
whole self
today?

MIND ●

BODY ●

SPIRIT ●

Write and release

Whatever is on your mind, write it out and let it go

_____

_____

_____

_____

I FEEL CALMER WITH EACH BREATH THAT I TAKE

How am I feeling today?

Colour in how full your heart is and write out any emotions you are feeling today

_____   ♡   _____

_____   _____

No matter how big or small . . .

What makes me happy?

_____

_____

_____

What are three good decisions I have made in the past six months?

_____

_____

_____

Have I taken care of my whole self today?

MIND ⬤

BODY ⬤

SPIRIT ⬤

Write and release

Whatever is on your mind, write it out and let it go

_____

_____

_____

_____

MINDFUL CHALLENGE

Challenge yourself to have a mindful day. Tick any of the below that you have managed to do recently. (One is left blank for you to fill in with something that is personal to you.)

EMBRACE THE SIGHTS AND SOUNDS OF NATURE

MAKE TIME TO FOCUS ON YOUR BREATH

NO SCREEN TIME BEFORE BED

JOURNAL YOUR THOUGHTS

GO FOR A WALK

READ A GOOD BOOK

I AM A PROGRESSION OF GREATNESS

How am I feeling today?

Colour in how full your heart is and write out any emotions you are feeling today

_____

_____

No matter how big or small . . .

I love spending my free time doing . . .

_____

_____

_____

What are parts of myself that I hide from others and why?

_____

_____

_____

Have I taken care of my whole self today?

MIND

BODY

SPIRIT

Write and release

Whatever is on your mind, write it out and let it go

_____

_____

_____

_____

I AM LOVING ALL THAT I AM BECOMING

How am I feeling today?

Colour in how full your heart is and write out any emotions you are feeling today

_____   ♡   _____
_____   _____

No matter how big or small . . .

What is a skill I am proud to have?

_____

_____

_____

What is something that means a lot to me that may not to others?

_____

_____

_____

Have I taken care of my whole self today?

MIND ●

BODY ●

SPIRIT ●

Write and release

Whatever is on your mind, write it out and let it go

_____

_____

_____

_____

I CHOOSE TO SEE BEAUTY IN ALL ASPECTS OF MY LIFE

How am I feeling today?

Colour in how full your heart is and write out any emotions you are feeling today

_____   ♡   _____
_____   _____

No matter how big or small . . .

The favourite part of my daily routine is . . .

_____

_____

Is it more important to love or be loved?

_____

_____

Have I taken care of my whole self today?

MIND 〇

BODY 〇

SPIRIT 〇

Write and release

Whatever is on your mind, write it out and let it go

_____

_____

_____

_____

MY SELF-LOVE LANGUAGE

 The longest relationship you will ever have is the one with yourself. Figuring out how to show yourself love is important, as this self-love language has a beautiful rippling effect into all other areas of your life. Gary Chapman was the pioneer behind the concept of love languages. What is your self-love language?

PHYSICAL TOUCH

Honouring your body by doing things that make it feel good.

Yoga asana, exercise, dancing, qigong, etc.

Massage or spa day

Epsom salt bath or warm shower

Skincare and grooming

Pampering sessions

RECEIVING GIFTS

Treating yourself or creating gifts for yourself that spark joy.

Spending money on your hobbies

Investing in knowledge and education

Going on a trip or holiday

Enjoying a nice meal out

QUALITY TIME

Scheduling uninterrupted alone time to nurture your being.

Meditation or introspection

Transformational breathing

Engaging in a creative passion

Spending time in nature

ACTS OF SERVICE

Doing tasks that need to be completed or things that have been neglected, which serve your well-being.

Making your bed

Taking the trash out

Preparing healthy meals

Scheduling, planning, organizing and delegating

WORDS OF AFFIRMATION

Positive self-talk, gratitude towards yourself, and empowering affirmations.

Speaking kindly to yourself

Listing your strengths and successes

Journaling and mantras

Speaking your ideal future into existence

I RISE ABOVE CHALLENGES AND OBSTACLES

How am I feeling today?

Colour in how full your heart is and write out any emotions you are feeling today

_____   _____
_____   _____

No matter how big or small . . .

Whose company do I enjoy the most?

_____

_____

_____

Whose approval do I seek the most and why?

_____

_____

_____

Have I taken care of my whole self today?

MIND ○

BODY ○

SPIRIT ○

Write and release

Whatever is on your mind, write it out and let it go

_____

_____

_____

_____

I FOCUS ON SOLUTIONS INSTEAD OF PROBLEMS

How am I feeling today?

Colour in how full your heart is and write out any emotions you are feeling today

No matter how big or small . . .

Who is my go-to person when I am feeling low?

To me, success means . . .

Have I taken
care of my
whole self
today?

MIND

BODY

SPIRIT

Write and release

Whatever is on your mind, write it out and let it go

I KEEP HOLD OF POSITIVE THOUGHTS AND FEELINGS

How am I feeling today?

Colour in how full your heart is and write out any emotions you are feeling today

_____ ♡ _____

_____ _____

No matter how big or small . . .

The kindest thing someone has ever said to me is . . .

_____

_____

_____

How can I show up more regularly for myself?

_____

_____

_____

Have I taken care of my whole self today?

MIND ⚪

BODY ⚪

SPIRIT ⚪

Write and release

Whatever is on your mind, write it out and let it go

_____

_____

_____

_____

AFFIRM IT

Affirming positive thoughts can have transformative effects. Write out
and repeat the affirmation below.

I AM KIND

I FEEL FRESH, REJUVENATED AND RECHARGED

How am I feeling today?
Colour in how full your heart is and write out any emotions you are feeling today

_____   ♡   _____
_____   _____

No matter how big or small . . .

I feel powerful when . . .

_____

_____

_____

Who is someone I wish I spent more time with and why?

_____

_____

_____

Have I taken care of my whole self today?

MIND ●

BODY ●

SPIRIT ●

Write and release
Whatever is on your mind, write it out and let it go

_____

_____

_____

I GIVE MYSELF SPACE TO GROW AND LEARN

How am I feeling today?

Colour in how full your heart is and write out any emotions you are feeling today

_____ ♡ _____
_____   _____

No matter how big or small . . .

When was the last time I truly enjoyed myself?

_____
_____
_____

What is something I could do forever and never get bored of?

_____
_____

Have I taken care of my whole self today?

MIND ●

BODY ●

SPIRIT ●

Write and release

Whatever is on your mind, write it out and let it go

_____
_____
_____
_____

WHAT IS MEANT FOR ME WILL ALWAYS FIND ITS WAY TO ME

How am I feeling today?

Colour in how full your heart is and write out any emotions you are feeling today

_____   _____

_____   _____

No matter how big or small . . .

My favourite way to ground myself is . . .

_____

_____

_____

When I envision my higher self, I see . . .

_____

_____

_____

Have I taken care of my whole self today?

MIND ●

BODY ●

SPIRIT ●

Write and release

Whatever is on your mind, write it out and let it go

_____

_____

_____

_____

MINDFUL COLOURING

 Colouring is a great way to get into a meditative state by calming the mind and feeling relaxed. Let your creativity flow and colour the below.

I AM BECOMING CLOSER TO MY TRUE SELF EVERY DAY

How am I feeling today?

Colour in how full your heart is and write out any emotions you are feeling today

_____   ♡   _____

_____   _____

No matter how big or small . . .

Something I have been putting off that I have finally done is . . .

_____

_____

_____

What is something I need to hear today?

_____

_____

_____

Have I taken care of my whole self today?

MIND ●

BODY ●

SPIRIT ●

Write and release

Whatever is on your mind, write it out and let it go

_____

_____

_____

_____

I AM VIBRATING HIGHER WITH EACH DAY THAT COMES

How am I feeling today?

Colour in how full your heart is and write out any emotions you are feeling today

_____ _____
_____ _____

No matter how big or small . . .

I feel confident when . . .

_____
_____
_____

Have I ever tried to change myself for someone and why?

_____
_____
_____

Have I taken care of my whole self today?

MIND

BODY

SPIRIT

Write and release

Whatever is on your mind, write it out and let it go

_____
_____
_____
_____

I CONSCIOUSLY RELEASE THE PAST AND LIVE IN THE PRESENT

How am I feeling today?

Colour in how full your heart is and write out any emotions you are feeling today

_____ ♡ _____

_____   _____

No matter how big or small . . .

What is something that helps me stay healthy?

_____

_____

_____

Am I getting enough sleep every night? If not, how can I improve on that?

_____

_____

_____

Have I taken care of my whole self today?

MIND ●

BODY ●

SPIRIT ●

Write and release

Whatever is on your mind, write it out and let it go

_____

_____

_____

_____

MY LIFE WHEEL

On a scale from 1 to 10, how am I feeling in the following areas of my life? Do not overthink it, just colour it in!

1 ——————————————————————— **10**

NOT-SO-GREAT   GREAT

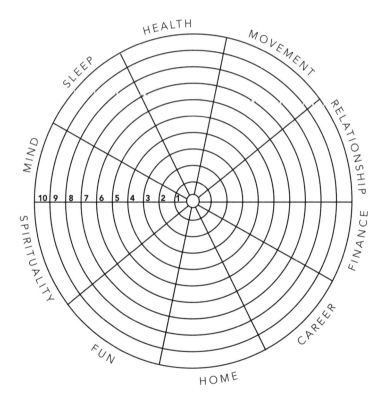

 Tip: *Use the space around the wheel to note ways in which you can add more balance to your life.*

I AM MINDFUL OF THE ENERGY I PUT OUT

How am I feeling today?

Colour in how full your heart is and write out any emotions you are feeling today

_____   _____

_____   _____

No matter how big or small . . .

What is something that makes me strive to do better?

_____

_____

_____

How do I remind myself that I am enough?

_____

_____

_____

Have I taken care of my whole self today?

MIND

BODY

SPIRIT

Write and release

Whatever is on your mind, write it out and let it go

_____

_____

_____

_____

I LEARN VALUABLE LIFE LESSONS EVERY DAY

How am I feeling today?

Colour in how full your heart is and write out any emotions you are feeling today

_____   _____

_____   _____

No matter how big or small . . .

My favourite moment of the day is . . .

_____

_____

_____

What is a different way I could compliment someone I love?

_____

_____

_____

Have I taken care of my whole self today?

MIND

BODY

SPIRIT

Write and release

Whatever is on your mind, write it out and let it go

_____

_____

_____

_____

I WELCOME ALL THAT IS MEANT FOR ME AND MORE

How am I feeling today?

Colour in how full your heart is and write out any emotions you are feeling today

_____   ♡   _____

_____   _____

No matter how big or small . . .

A quality that I love about myself is . . .

_____

_____

_____

Something I need to do less of and something I need to do more of is . . .

_____

_____

_____

Have I taken care of my whole self today?

MIND ●

BODY ●

SPIRIT ●

Write and release

Whatever is on your mind, write it out and let it go

_____

_____

_____

_____

I LOVE THAT I . . .

Write what you are, the things you can do, and the things you have. This is a great exercise for gratitude.

AM	CAN	HAVE

WHEN I LET GO, I CREATE SPACE FOR SOMETHING BETTER

How am I feeling today?

Colour in how full your heart is and write out any emotions you are feeling today

_____   _____

_____   _____

No matter how big or small . . .

A dream of mine that has come true is . . .

_____

_____

_____

What is the kindest thing I have done for a stranger?

_____

_____

_____

Have I taken care of my whole self today?

MIND ●

BODY ●

SPIRIT ●

Write and release

Whatever is on your mind, write it out and let it go

_____

_____

_____

_____

I AM READY FOR ALL THE BLESSINGS THAT ARE COMING MY WAY

How am I feeling today?

Colour in how full your heart is and write out any emotions you are feeling today

_____ _____
_____ _____

No matter how big or small . . .

What is something I have seen or heard today that I am grateful for?

_____

_____

_____

What is a moment that changed my life for the better, and how?

_____

_____

_____

Have I taken care of my whole self today?

MIND ⬤

BODY ⬤

SPIRIT ⬤

Write and release

Whatever is on your mind, write it out and let it go

_____

_____

_____

_____

I AM THANKFUL FOR MY MISTAKES AS THEY HAVE MADE ME WHO I AM TODAY

How am I feeling today?

Colour in how full your heart is and write out any emotions you are feeling today

_____   _____

No matter how big or small . . .

Who is someone that I am grateful to have loved?

_____

_____

_____

What do I do when I feel sad? Does it benefit me or hinder me?

_____

_____

_____

Have I taken care of my whole self today?

MIND

BODY

SPIRIT

Write and release

Whatever is on your mind, write it out and let it go

_____

_____

_____

_____

GRATITUDE IS THE ATTITUDE

 Finding gratitude in everyday life is a recipe for feeling great. There are so many beautiful things, people and lessons to be grateful for. Open up your heart and mind to feel the positive impact of counting your blessings below.

I AM GRATEFUL FOR . . .

1 place

1 skill

1 song

1 lesson

1 person

1 feeling

1 memory

1 experience

1 compliment

1 self-care act

1 quality of mine

1 piece of advice

I APPRECIATE WHERE I AM GOING IN MY LIFE

How am I feeling today?

Colour in how full your heart is and write out any emotions you are feeling today

_____   _____

No matter how big or small . . .

What is one positive word I can use to describe myself?

_____

_____

_____

I am worth knowing because . . .

_____

_____

_____

Have I taken care of my whole self today?

MIND ⬤

BODY ⬤

SPIRIT ⬤

Write and release

Whatever is on your mind, write it out and let it go

_____

_____

_____

_____

THERE IS ONLY ROOM FOR LOVE AND KINDNESS IN MY HEART

How am I feeling today?

Colour in how full your heart is and write out any emotions you are feeling today

No matter how big or small . . .

The last time I felt good about myself was . . .

Are my recent choices helping my happiness?

Have I taken care of my whole self today?

MIND

BODY

SPIRIT

Write and release

Whatever is on your mind, write it out and let it go

EVERYTHING IS ALWAYS WORKING OUT FOR MY GREATEST GOOD

How am I feeling today?

Colour in how full your heart is and write out any emotions you are feeling today

_____   _____

_____   _____

No matter how big or small . . .

If all my dreams come true a year from now, what will I be grateful for?

_____

_____

_____

Is there a trait I see in others that I wish I had myself?

_____

_____

_____

Have I taken care of my whole self today?

MIND

BODY

SPIRIT

Write and release
Whatever is on your mind, write it out and let it go

_____

_____

_____

_____

COLOURING QUOTE

Colouring is a great way to get into a meditative state by calming the mind and feeling relaxed. Visualize and feel the words below as you colour.

I AM COMFORTABLE IN MY OWN SKIN

How am I feeling today?

Colour in how full your heart is and write out any emotions you are feeling today

_____   _____

_____   _____

No matter how big or small . . .

My favourite way to celebrate myself or an achievement is . . .

_____

_____

_____

What is a hobby/activity that I love but do not get enough time for?

_____

_____

_____

Have I taken care of my whole self today?

MIND ●

BODY ●

SPIRIT ●

Write and release

Whatever is on your mind, write it out and let it go

_____

_____

_____

_____

I AM MY OWN KIND OF BEAUTIFUL

How am I feeling today?

Colour in how full your heart is and write out any emotions you are feeling today

No matter how big or small . . .

A time I felt thrilled was . . .

What does it feel like when I slow down?

Have I taken
care of my
whole self
today?

MIND

BODY

SPIRIT

Write and release

Whatever is on your mind, write it out and let it go

I ALLOW GOOD THOUGHTS AND ENERGIES TO NOURISH MY SPACE

How am I feeling today?

Colour in how full your heart is and write out any emotions you are feeling today

_____   ♡   _____
_____   _____

No matter how big or small . . .

One thing I love about my home is . . .

_____

_____

_____

If I had the day to myself, what would I do?

_____

_____

_____

Have I taken care of my whole self today?

MIND ⬤

BODY ⬤

SPIRIT ⬤

Write and release

Whatever is on your mind, write it out and let it go

_____

_____

_____

_____

RESET YOUR SPACE

 They say a tidy space reflects a tidy mind. Be sure to set some time aside every so often to keep on top of your surroundings and refresh your environment.

DO YOUR LAUNDRY

GET YOUR DIARY ORGANIZED

DECLUTTER YOUR WARDROBE

SORT OUT YOUR HOME ADMIN

CLEAN OUT YOUR FRIDGE/ PANTRY

CLEAN UP YOUR PHYSICAL SPACE

CLEANSE/ CHARGE YOUR CRYSTALS

STOCK UP ON YOUR HOME ESSENTIALS

TAKE A DEEP DIVE INTO YOUR FINANCES

 Tip: Try adding your favourite way to reset to your Calm Kit (page 22).

MIRACLES AND BLESSINGS SURROUND ME IN EVERY MOMENT

How am I feeling today?

Colour in how full your heart is and write out any emotions you are feeling today

_____   ♡   _____

_____   _____

No matter how big or small . . .

My favourite feeling is when . . .

_____

_____

_____

What advice do I give to others but do not follow myself?

_____

_____

_____

Have I taken care of my whole self today?

MIND ⬤

BODY ⬤

SPIRIT ⬤

Write and release

Whatever is on your mind, write it out and let it go

_____

_____

_____

_____

I INVEST MY ENERGY WHERE IT FEELS RIGHT FOR ME

How am I feeling today?

Colour in how full your heart is and write out any emotions you are feeling today

No matter how big or small . . .

My mind is most focused when . . .

How can I show someone I love them with my actions and not words?

Have I taken care of my whole self today?

MIND

BODY

SPIRIT

Write and release

Whatever is on your mind, write it out and let it go

I ALLOW MYSELF TO FEEL AND RELEASE ANY UNHELPFUL EMOTIONS

How am I feeling today?

Colour in how full your heart is and write out any emotions you are feeling today

_____   ♡   _____
_____   _____

No matter how big or small . . .

What do I do every day that makes me happy?

_____

_____

_____

If I had three wishes, I would wish for . . .

_____

_____

_____

Have I taken care of my whole self today?

MIND ●

BODY ●

SPIRIT ●

Write and release

Whatever is on your mind, write it out and let it go

_____

_____

_____

_____

I LOVE MYSELF

When was the last time you truly appreciated your existence? There are so many beautiful things about you that go unnoticed. Dig a little deeper and write down fifteen things you love about yourself.

1
2
3
4
5
6
7
8
9
10
11
12
13
14
15

 Tip: Add this exercise to your Calm Kit (page 22).

I AM UNAFFECTED BY THE JUDGEMENTS OF OTHERS

How am I feeling today?

Colour in how full your heart is and write out any emotions you are feeling today

_____   _____
_____   _____

No matter how big or small . . .

One movie that puts me in a good mood is . . .

_____

_____

_____

Is there someone or something I need to forgive in my life?

_____

_____

_____

Have I taken care of my whole self today?

MIND 〇

BODY 〇

SPIRIT 〇

Write and release
Whatever is on your mind, write it out and let it go

_____

_____

_____

_____

I CHOOSE TO RESPOND WITH KINDNESS AND WISDOM

How am I feeling today?

Colour in how full your heart is and write out any emotions you are feeling today

No matter how big or small . . .

A book that brings me joy is . . .

Three emotions that I tend to feel most of the time are . . .

Have I taken care of my whole self today?

MIND

BODY

SPIRIT

Write and release

Whatever is on your mind, write it out and let it go

I GROW IN CONFIDENCE AND CLARITY DAILY

How am I feeling today?

Colour in how full your heart is and write out any emotions you are feeling today

_____   ♡   _____
_____   _____

No matter how big or small . . .

What do I have to look forward to tomorrow?

_____

_____

_____

The last time I tried something new, it made me feel . . .

_____

_____

_____

Have I taken
care of my
whole self
today?

MIND ●

BODY ●

SPIRIT ●

Write and release

Whatever is on your mind, write it out and let it go

_____

_____

_____

_____

LOVE CHALLENGE

Challenge yourself to share some love. Tick any of the below that you have managed to do recently. (One is left blank for you to fill in with something that is personal to you.)

GIVE SOMEONE
A HUG

OFFER TO DO
SOMETHING FOR
A LOVED ONE

GIVE SOMEONE
A COMPLIMENT

MESSAGE A
LOVED ONE

GIVE YOUR TIME
TO SOMEONE IN
NEED

COOK A MEAL FOR
A LOVED ONE

THERE IS ALWAYS SPACE FOR ME IN THIS UNIVERSE

How am I feeling today?

Colour in how full your heart is and write out any emotions you are feeling today

_____

_____

_____

_____

No matter how big or small . . .

My body feels nourished when . . .

_____

_____

_____

I need to say 'no' more often to . . .

_____

_____

_____

Have I taken care of my whole self today?

MIND ⬤

BODY ⬤

SPIRIT ⬤

Write and release

Whatever is on your mind, write it out and let it go

_____

_____

_____

_____

I AM SAFE IN THIS MOMENT

How am I feeling today?

Colour in how full your heart is and write out any emotions you are feeling today

No matter how big or small . . .

I am ambitious about . . .

I need to say 'yes' more often to . . .

Have I taken care of my whole self today?

MIND

BODY

SPIRIT

Write and release

Whatever is on your mind, write it out and let it go

PEACE PERVADES MY BEING IN EVERY MOMENT

How am I feeling today?

Colour in how full your heart is and write out any emotions you are feeling today

_____   _____
_____   _____

No matter how big or small . . .

My perfect day looks like . . .

_____

_____

_____

What is my purpose in life?

_____

_____

_____

Have I taken care of my whole self today?

MIND ⬤

BODY ⬤

SPIRIT ⬤

Write and release

Whatever is on your mind, write it out and let it go

_____

_____

_____

PRANAYAMA

Practising pranayama (or breathwork) can help improve your well-being and bring a state of calmness to your mind. Why not try these three controlled breathwork techniques to help balance your body and mind?

ALTERNATE NOSTRIL BREATHING

Nadi Shodhana

With your right thumb, close your right nostril

Exhale through your left nostril

Pause gently

Inhale through your left nostril

With your ring and pinky finger, close your left nostril

Exhale through your right nostril

Pause gently

Inhale through your right nostril

With your right thumb, close your right nostril

REPEAT x 10

RIGHT NOSTRIL BREATHING

Surya Bheda

With your ring and pinky finger, close your left nostril

Inhale through your right nostril

With your right thumb, close your right nostril

Exhale through your left nostril

With your ring and pinky finger, close your left nostril

REPEAT x 10

HUMMING BEE BREATHING

Bhramari Pranayama

Apply pressure on your ears with your index fingers to block out any sound

Close your eyes

Take a deep breath in

Exhale and make a humming sound like a bee while gently pressing the cartilage

Inhale again and continue the same process

REPEAT x 10

MY UNDERSTANDING IS EXPANDING WITH EACH BREATH I TAKE

How am I feeling today?
Colour in how full your heart is and write out any emotions you are feeling today

_____   _____
_____   _____

No matter how big or small . . .

A time I was surrounded by love was . . .

_____

_____

_____

How do I prioritize my mental health?

_____

_____

_____

Have I taken care of my whole self today?

MIND

BODY

SPIRIT

Write and release
Whatever is on your mind, write it out and let it go

_____

_____

_____

_____

I ALLOW MYSELF TO LIVE A HEALTHY LIFE

How am I feeling today?

Colour in how full your heart is and write out any emotions you are feeling today

No matter how big or small . . .

What is something kind I can say to myself right now?

An accomplishment my younger self would have been proud of is . . .

Have I taken care of my whole self today?

MIND

BODY

SPIRIT

Write and release

Whatever is on your mind, write it out and let it go

I AM FORTUNATE TO EXPERIENCE ANOTHER BLISSFUL DAY

How am I feeling today?

Colour in how full your heart is and write out any emotions you are feeling today

_____

No matter how big or small . . .

I am grateful that I can . . .

_____

What is something I wish I could experience?

_____

Have I taken care of my whole self today?

MIND

BODY

SPIRIT

Write and release

Whatever is on your mind, write it out and let it go

BUCKET LIST BREAKDOWN

It is time to take action on your bucket list. What are the next three things you want to tick off yours? Break them down to make them achievable in the near future!

1
....

ACTION PLAN

2
....

ACTION PLAN

3
....

ACTION PLAN

I LET MY ENERGY DRIVE ME TO SOMETHING BIGGER AND BETTER

How am I feeling today?

Colour in how full your heart is and write out any emotions you are feeling today

_____ _____

_____ _____

No matter how big or small . . .

When I am happy I . . .

_____

_____

_____

A moment that has challenged me is . . .

_____

_____

_____

Have I taken care of my whole self today?

MIND ●

BODY ●

SPIRIT ●

Write and release

Whatever is on your mind, write it out and let it go

_____

_____

_____

_____

MY MIND IS BRILLIANT AND MY SOUL IS LUMINOUS

How am I feeling today?

Colour in how full your heart is and write out any emotions you are feeling today

_____   _____

_____   _____

No matter how big or small . . .

Five things I am grateful for are . . .

_____

_____

_____

When was the last time I put myself first?

_____

_____

_____

Have I taken care of my whole self today?

MIND

BODY

SPIRIT

Write and release

Whatever is on your mind, write it out and let it go

_____

_____

_____

_____

I AM HEALING. I AM GROWING. I AM WHOLE.

How am I feeling today?

Colour in how full your heart is and write out any emotions you are feeling today

_____   ♡   _____
_____   _____

No matter how big or small . . .

The biggest lesson I have learned so far in my life is . . .

_____

_____

_____

What is something I feel no one understands about me?

_____

_____

_____

Have I taken care of my whole self today?

MIND ●

BODY ●

SPIRIT ●

Write and release

Whatever is on your mind, write it out and let it go

_____

_____

_____

_____

WRITE A LETTER TO YOUR YOUNGER SELF

 This exercise is a therapeutic way to recognize what your younger self needed to hear. What would you say and what advice would you give?

Dear younger self,

I AM CREATING A POSITIVE FUTURE FOR MYSELF

How am I feeling today?

Colour in how full your heart is and write out any emotions you are feeling today

_____   ♡   _____
_____   _____

No matter how big or small . . .

Who is someone I highly respect and why?

_____

_____

_____

What would I do if I knew I could not fail?

_____

_____

_____

Have I taken care of my whole self today?

MIND ●

BODY ●

SPIRIT ●

Write and release

Whatever is on your mind, write it out and let it go

_____

_____

_____

_____

I HAVE THE STRENGTH TO GET THROUGH ALL THAT IS HAPPENING TO ME

How am I feeling today?

Colour in how full your heart is and write out any emotions you are feeling today

_____   _____

_____   _____

No matter how big or small . . .

My mind feels nourished when . . .

_____

_____

_____

When I look in the mirror, I feel . . .

_____

_____

_____

Have I taken care of my whole self today?

MIND

BODY

SPIRIT

Write and release

Whatever is on your mind, write it out and let it go

_____

_____

_____

_____

MY REFLECTIONS

THIS JOURNAL HAS TAUGHT ME . . .

SOMETHING I HAVE LEARNT ABOUT MYSELF IS . . .

I AM PROUD OF MYSELF BECAUSE . . .

I WISH I DID MORE OF . . .

I WISH I DID LESS OF . . .

MY REFLECTIONS

WERE THERE ANY MISTAKES I MADE?

WERE THERE ANY LIFE-CHANGING MOMENTS FOR ME?

MY BIGGEST ACHIEVEMENT HAS BEEN . . .

NOW THE BIG QUESTION... WHAT'S NEXT?

NOTES

NOTES

NOTES

NOTES

I AM SO PROUD OF HOW FAR
I HAVE COME BUT THE REST
IS STILL UNWRITTEN...